TH
HOUSE DATER'S
TOOLKIT

John Chapman

THE

HOUSE DATER'S

TOOLKIT

First published 1998, reprinted 2002

ISBN 1 900038 15 3

Published & printed by

GLEN GRAPHICS

4 Ryecroft Park, Wooler, Northumberland NE71 6AS
Tel/Fax: 01668 281249

Email: info@glengraphics.co.uk
Web: www.glengraphics.co.uk

Dedication

To my wife, for help in making the house dating game so much fun over so many miles and in so many places.

Contents

Note Throughout the text, numbers placed in brackets refer to
boks listed in the Bibliography at the end of each chapter.

The Author

John Chapman is a retired physicist whose varied industrial career led him steadily northwards. With his wife, he renovated three old country houses as he progressed, gaining those detailed insights into vernacular architecture which have informed his thinking in writing this book. A datestone on their present house in Hexham declares its date to be 1770, but old hinges, wood-pegged lintels and similar small details led to an earlier date of 1656. The obvious interest of many friends in the deductions which could be made from clues of this sort led to several winters of research, interspersed with summer travels to view dated houses. The resulting comprehensive collection of dateable features from houses of many types is presented as the House Dater's Tool Kit.

Privacy

Except where advertised as open to the public, all of the buildings mentioned or illustrated in this book are in private occupation and readers are asked to respect that privacy.

Acknowledgements

I wish to acknowledge my thanks to the many authors whose works are listed in the bibliographies; without pointers gleaned from their ideas, the task would have been too great. I am also indebted to those kind owners who have generously allowed us to study the interiors and exteriors of their houses in our search for clues. Finally, but not least, I must thank those members of my family, especially Emma, who leapt to the aid of a computer-illiterate to type my final manuscript.

John Chapman
High Shield
1998

Introduction

The only certain way to date a house is by finding relevant deeds, records or maps which give unequivocal dates. In the absence of such documents, the external and internal appearance of the house may be used to make an informed guess at the date of its erection and later alterations. Sash windows, set in a symmetrical facade, would suggest a Georgian date, but by noting that the glazing bars were thick, and the top sashes of each window were fixed, it would be possible to narrow the date to somewhere early in the Georgian period. If it was then noted that the house failed to achieve complete symmetry, because only one of the two chimney stacks was placed at the end of the roof ridge, this would suggest that the Georgian facade was a re-facing of an earlier building. This idea would be supported if the interior revealed a dog-leg staircase with shallow treads and splat balusters, which could indicate a date in the seventeenth century. By combining the many clues which can be seen, it is possible to build up an approximate history of a house, showing the changes which have taken place as each owner sought to put his individual imprint on the building. The problem is to know which clues are of significance for dating, and the dates to which they correspond.

This book aims to present the dating information, gratefully acknowledged from many authors quoted in the bibliography, as a series of pictures of what can be seen on or in houses of many ages. Each picture has notes on the approximate date range during which that particular type of window, door or hinge, etc. was in general use. It will be argued that it is not possible to do this, because fashions were adopted at different times in different parts of the country. It is sometimes stated that fashions took one hundred years to move from the south of England to the north. In fact it was the conservatism of the people in the Pennines and the north west of England which led them to choose not to adopt the newfangled styles, sometimes for as much as a hundred years, but elsewhere in the country a study of dated houses and their features shows that the transmission of new ideas was very rapid, sometimes from north to south, rather than the reverse. Celia Fiennes' Journals c.1700 show that, wherever she travelled, people were installing the new sash windows, or the latest form of room panelling; ideas were rapidly disseminated in the eighteenth century, and later, by architects' pattern books, and nation-wide journals such as the Gentlemen's Magazine. As early as 1591 a gable end very similar to that at Bourne Mill (Gable Ends, Fig.3) was to be seen one year later in Heidelberg.

Nevertheless, there must clearly be regional differences in dating. This book should be used as a key to be compared with houses of known date in a given region; this will establish the date shift likely to be noted for features in that region. Suggestions from readers for correcting the proposed date ranges with dates from their regions would be most welcome for any future publications.If any regional bias is noted, it will be towards examples from the north east of England, and in particular the Hexham area. The plea is made that these areas have been neglected in vernacular studies, and they are the areas in which much of this work was carried out. Many of the findings have been confirmed by extended journeys throughout England, seeking out the pleasures of old buildings which anyone can enjoy if they will open their eyes.

When a house has been thoroughly studied, and the date ranges have been noted corresponding to different features, it is useful to represent these results visually.

On thefollowing page we consider a hypothetical northern house and note its features.The result is fairly typical, in that the features of the side and interior of the house suggest a date in the early seventeenth century for the earliest house. Around 1700 the front facade was given an appearance of symmetry, but the windows were probably the twin-light mullioned type, the date being just too early for the adoption of sash windows. Although the Yorkshire sash is reputed to have been introduced in 1705, it took upwards of twenty years to move far from its origin, and so it is assumed that later in the eighteenth century the mullions were removed and the horizontally-sliding Yorkshire sashes were inserted. This could be confirmed if traces of the removal of the mullion could be seen. A very useful treatment of the logic process involved in dating buildings is to be found in Investigating Old Buildings by L. Smith (1985).

Details of a hypothetical Northern house

Feature	Date Range			
	1500	1600	1700	1800
Front of house				
Door:				
Swan-necked, split pediment			c.1685 — c1715	
Bolection surround			c.1680 — c. 1710	
Windows:				
Square surround			c. 1680 - c. 1700	
Yorkshire sash			c. 1705	
Side of house				
Door:				
Tudor arch	15C		c.1750	
Windows:				
4-light mullioned		16C	c1730 (In some areas).	
Interior				
Main staircase:				
Splat balusters		c1600 .... c1650		
Plain square newels		Late 16C	c1730	

BRICK

Brick was widely obtainable by the fifteenth century in stoneless counties (16), and it was accepted for the finest buildings by 1500; its use gradually spread to yeoman houses throughout the sixteenth century. Ten houses were named Brickhouse Farm c.1600 in Essex (1), indicating that brick was still uncommon in the area. Small brick houses were built from c.1650, and by the middle of the eighteenth century brick was the most commonly used material for small buildings. Exposed brick was unpopular by the end of that century, and it was normally rendered with stucco to such an extent that, between 1820 and 1840, brick seemed to be disappearing from use. It came into favour again after the middle of the century; polychromy, with facades incorporating bricks of different colours, and red bricks in the Queen Anne revival, were two of the fashions, and brick has been the commonest material for small buildings ever since.

In trying to date a brick building it is necessary to study local practice, as the pattern of use varied widely around the country. London and Newcastle largely replaced timber buildings with brick in the seventeenth century, and major fires led to re-building in brick in Marlborough (1653), Northampton (1675) and Morpeth (1689) to name but a few. A useful dating summary for brick is given by Iredale and Barrett (6).

Visual dating of brickwork is very approximate at best. There is, as yet, no scientific dating method analogous to carbon dating for wood or thermoluminescence for pottery. Brick sizes, colour and texture, and the pattern, called bonding, in which bricks are laid in a wall, can be studied, as well as stylistic features such as diaper patterns and ornamental chimneys, for which approximate dates of occurrence are known.

Table 1 - Brick Sizes

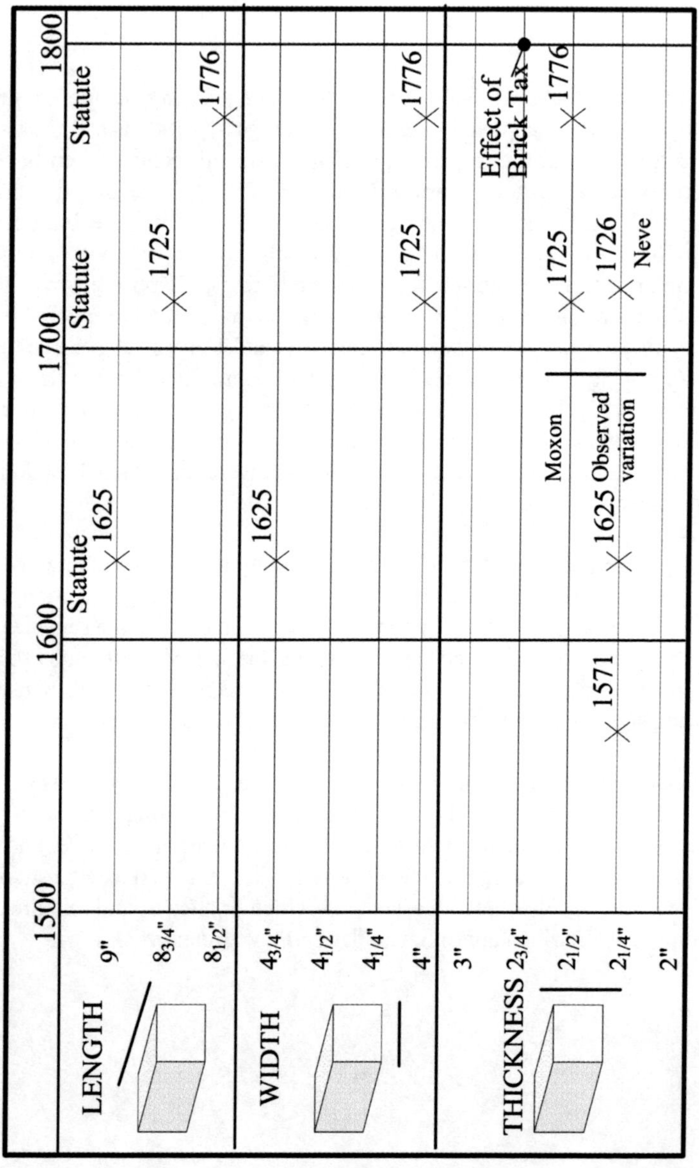

	1500	1600	1700	1800
LENGTH 9"		Statute 1625 ✕		
8¾"			Statute 1725 ✕	
8½"				Statute 1776 ✕
WIDTH 4¾"		1625 ✕		
4½"				
4¼"			1725 ✕	1776 ✕
4"				
THICKNESS 3"				
2¾"	1571 ✕	Moxon / 1625 ✕ Observed variation	1725 ✕	1776 ✕
2½"			Effect of Brick Tax ●	
2¼"			1726 ✕ Neve	
2"				

Brick sizes (Table 1)

Variations in clay quality and the control of firing temperatures led to wide variations in brick dimensions. In addition, there appears to have been little standardisation of sizes between different localities. In the Brick Dating Summary which follows, variations in size from the twelfth to the sixteenth century will be seen to have been considerable. After the Brickmakers Charter of 1571, statutes were passed specifying standard brick sizes, but they do not appear to have been followed closely. Writers on building matters appeared to disregard the statutes; Moxon (1677) (9) recommended 2½" thick bricks, and Neve (11) in 1726 suggested 2¼". The main trend was a gradual increase in thickness from c. 2" in 1500, to 2¼" in 1571. An Act of 1625 specified brick sizes of 9" x 4¾" x 2¼" (12), but thicknesses varied from 2" to 25/8" until 1725, when a further Act specified 8¾" x 4" x 2½" (5). The next change was an Act of 1776 specifying sizes of 8½" x 4" x 2½" (12). A Brick Tax, introduced in 1784, taxed the number of bricks used on a building; the obvious response was to reduce building costs by producing thicker bricks, and thicknesses gradually increased to 3". An analysis of brick dimensions, from different times and locations, listed by Lloyd (7) shows that sizes tended to be smaller than the size specified in the statute current at the time of manufacture. This practice gave a commercial gain when bricks were sold by quantity rather than by size, but it could have been due to poor quality control. For success in dating a building, it is necessary to make comparisons with local dated brick buildings, as no national size guide can be given.

Surface Features

Early bricks were fired in clamps, using poorly mixed clays, and the resulting product was frequently misshapen, showing small pebbles, pits, poorly mixed clay and other materials in its surface. Standards improved slowly during the eighteenth century, but it was not until mechanical brick-making started c.1820 that reasonably uniform products were developed. Other major improvements came with the technique of heavy pressing in 1831, and with wire-cut brick manufacture after 1850.

From the time of Henry VIII, crimson bricks were common, resulting from insufficiently fired clay, and red was the predominant colour until the early eighteenth century. Colours could vary from red through plum to purple, and finally blue, depending on the position of the brick in the clamp or kiln. Where the ends of bricks, called headers, were over-burnt to

Table 2 - Brick colours

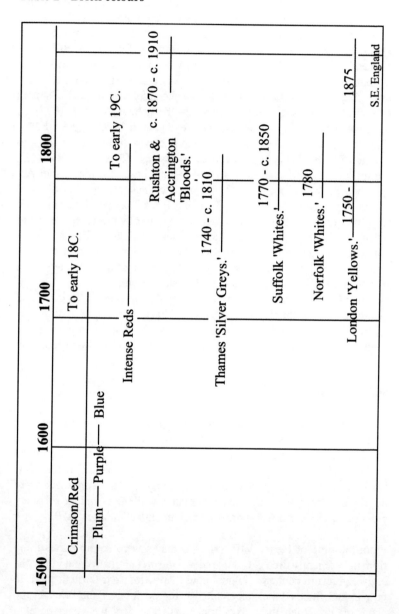

a dark blue colour, they were used to form diaper patterns which occurred as early as c.1434 at Bardney Church near Tattershall (17), and patterned brickwork was very common from about 1470 (Fig.1); good examples can be seen at the Bishop's Palace in Hatfield c.1480, and Farnham Castle in

Fig 1.

Surrey (1472-75) (3). This fashion peaked in the early sixteenth century. Bright orange bricks were used for gauged work in which the bricks were carefully shaped and laid with very fine mortar joints. This technique became popular c.1660 after the Restoration. The gauged work contrasted the dressings of the windows with the surrounding rougher red bricks. Intense red bricks were produced in the Midlands for a hundred years from the early eighteenth century. They were again popular from 1870 to the early twentieth century when Ruabon and Accrington bloods were produced, fuelling the Queen Anne revival (10). These led to a comment, which I once heard, describing the architectural periods of Southport in Lancashire, as bloody and late-bloody from the intense coloration of the brickwork.

From about 1740 it became fashionable to use bricks with colours approximating to those of stone, and they were often used in conjunction with stone dressings. So-called white bricks were used as early as the late fifteenth century in Jesus College, Cambridge (3), but regular production did not come until the eighteenth century. Chalk in the clay contributed to the light colour of the bricks. Silver-greys were produced in the Thames valley between 1740 and c.1810 (6). Pale grey bricks, referred to as whites, came from Suffolk between 1770 and 1850, and Norfolk production of white bricks began c.1780. Yellow bricks, commonly known as London stocks, were used almost exclusively in London between 1750 and 1875 (5), and they appeared in much of south-east England in the early twentieth century. Muthesius (10) and Clifton-Taylor (3) should be consulted for detailed information on the dating of coloured bricks. Table 2 summarises the date ranges for the different colours.

Multi-coloured brickwork became fashionable in larger buildings in the middle of the nineteenth century, with smaller buildings following the trend in the last thirty years of the century. In Northumberland, there are only minor outbreaks of banding or patterning in two colours from this period; in particular, yellow bricks became common for chimney stacks, and sometimes for complete houses in this area around 1880. Interestingly, the use of patterning with coloured bricks has been undergoing a revival from c.1985.

Bonding refers to the manner in which bricks are arranged in a wall to give different strengths and decorative effects. At first, it does not seem to have been fully appreciated that it is necessary to add strength to a brick wall by tying the outer skin of bricks to those further in, by placing some bricks in the header position. Such a brick ties the outer layer of bricks to those further in. As headers are placed at regular intervals, a pattern develops, called the bond. Examples of haphazard bonding occurred up to the end of the seventeenth century. Of the many bonds known, only those for which dating information has been found are discussed. Fuller details of these and other, undated bonds can be found in the bibliography, especially Brunskill (2) and Brian (15). Anthea Brian's distribution maps are reproduced with minor additions as Appendix 1.

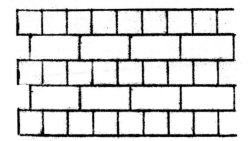

English bond (Fig.2) may have originated in France. It was systematically used at Tattershall Castle, which was completed in 1449.

Fig 2.

Flemish bond (Fig.3) was known in the fourteenth century, but it came into general use after its adoption for the Dutch House which was built at Kew in 1631 (13). By the reign of Queen Anne, Flemish bond was displacing the use of English bond in many areas. English bond remained popular in the north-east, and it regained favour for Gothic and structural work in the nineteenth century.

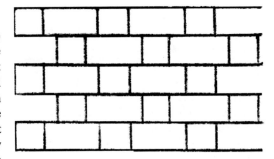

Fig 3.

English Garden Wall bond (Fig.4) was noted in 1559 (12), and it came into common use in the seventeenth century. It remained popular in the north-east of England in the nineteenth century, when Flemish bond was penetrating the north-west in Carlisle.

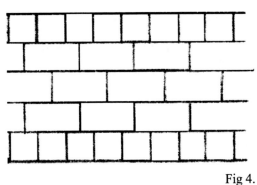

Fig 4.

Some localities used three courses of stretchers to one of headers, while

15

others, but a few miles away, used five stretcher courses. Some early eighteenth century work shows eight, nine or ten courses of stretchers to one of headers in the same wall. This bond was almost universal in the north-east for solid brickwork, other bonds being rare and confined to better class houses.

Flemish Garden Wall bond (Fig.5) came into use about the middle of the sixteenth century (15) with two, three or five stretchers being used to each header along a course (6). This bond was less expensive in its use of headers than the stronger English and Flemish bonds. It was

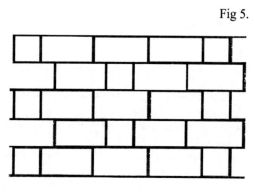

Fig 5.

not used in Georgian facades because it limited freedom in the spacing of windows.

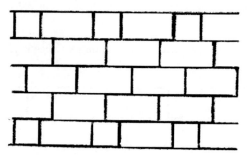

Flemish Stretcher bond (Fig.6) was noted as early as 1564 (15), and it occurred in the north-east in a few locations in the late eighteenth century.

Fig 6.

Header bond (Fig.7) is seen mainly in Berkshire, Hampshire and the south-east of England in eighteenth century buildings, although outliers can be found in Darlington in the north-east. This bond used the many bricks, having one end fired with an attractive blue colour, which resulted from firing irregularities in the wood-fired kilns. This bond persisted into the nineteenth century, and is still used for curved walls.

Fig 7.

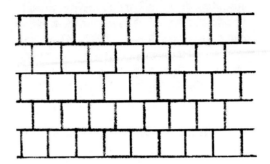

Fig 8.

Dearne's bond (Fig.8) was used in the late eighteenth century and the early nineteenth. It consisted of courses of headers alternating with courses of brick on edge. This bond produced a wall with a three-inch cavity, tied by the rows of headers. It was mainly used in humbler buildings.

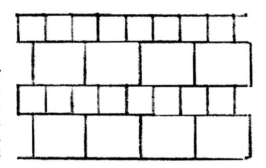

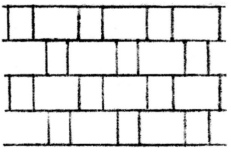

Rat-trap bond (Fig.9) looks like Flemish bond, but the bricks are all laid on edge. It produces a cheap cavity wall, and was used in the nineteenth and twentieth centuries.

Fig 9.

Stretcher bond (Fig.10) is nowadays the usual bond for cavity walls. In the absence of headers, the outer skin of the wall is fixed with metal ties to the inner skin. Cavity walls of this type came into use c.1905 (14), and this bond has been the most commonly used throughout the twentieth century. However, it did occur much earlier for the re-facing of buildings, examples having been seen which probably date from the early eighteenth century.

Local bonds, which are not nationally recognised, can represent the work of one or two craftsmen over their working lives (Fig.11), and can occasionally provide some local dating information.

Fig 10.   Fig 11.

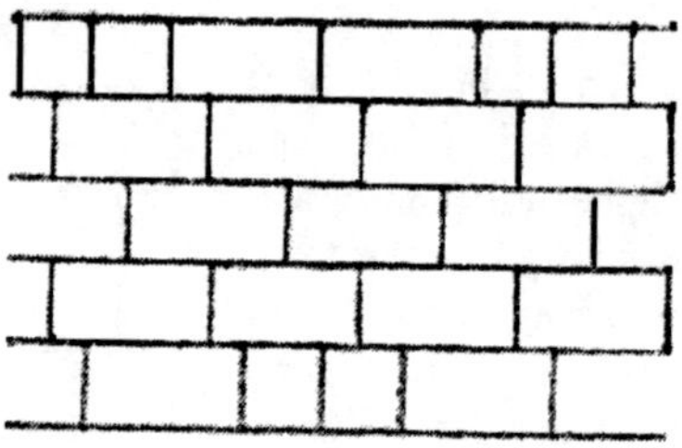

Brick Dating Summary

12C to 14C	'Great Bricks' occurred in Essex (13" x 6" x 2"). Mainly ecclesiastical work (16).
Late 13C onwards	Brick sizes were most usually 9" to 91/2" x 4" to 41/2" x 4" to 41/2" x 2" to 21/4" (16).
14C	Bricks of 10" x 5" x 21/2" occurred in Norfolk (16).
14C to 15C	In Northern cities (Hull, York etc.) bricks of size 10" to 11" x 5" to 51/2" x 11/2" to 21/4" were in use.
15C	Brick chimneys began to be built in town houses and larger houses in East Anglia (3).
1410	Diaper patterns used in brickwork at Stoner Park, Oxon (16). These patterns common by 1470.

1450	English bond used at Tattershall Castle.
1470 to 1500	The use of elaborate brick chimneys very common. This fashion was exhausted by 1520 (16). Spiral chimneys built from c.1485. Corbel tables with trefoil and cinquefoil ornamentation appeared.
c.1500	Brick chimneys began to be built for medium-sized country houses. They were seldom seen for small houses before the reign of Elizabeth I (3).
1505	Brick size of 10" x 5" x 21/2" noted (16).
1530	Brick size of 91/2" x 43/4" x 23/8" noted (16).
16C	Brick gables built in conjunction with timber-framed walls.
Late 16C	The first all-brick smaller houses were built. Brick walls before 1600 were generally one and a half bricks thick, giving a wall thickness of fourteen inches (1).
1559	English Garden Wall bond first noted.
1625	Act passed to regulate brick sizes to 9" x 43/4" x 21/4".
1631	Flemish bond used in Kew Palace. Brick tumbling on a dated barn wall of 1631 (4) may be the earliest example of tumbling noted. Rusticated brickwork was used on the Dutch House in London. This practice became common through to the eighteenth century on larger buildings.
c.1650	Smallish houses built entirely of brick were seen from this date, and by the last quarter of the seventeenth century low status brick houses became common.
1670	Many forms of decorative brickwork became fashionable, such as string courses, toothed eaves

cornices, cut and moulded bricks, rubbed brick arches, brick quoins and curvilinear gables. The latter fell from popularity c.1720, but the other features were in evidence well into the eighteenth century. By the late eighteenth century, eaves cornices were simplified from two courses of brick to a single course (5). The use of rubbed brick arches declined in London from the Regency, and from most other parts by 1850.

1676	Moxon (9) recommended that bricks should be 2½" thick.
c.1700	Red brick production commenced in quantity in the Midlands, continuing to the end of the century.
1725	Neve (11) recommended that bricks should be 2¼" thick. An Act was passed to regulate brick sizes to 8¾" x 4" x 2½".
1740	Stone-coloured bricks popular for the next hundred years. Production of Thames valley silver-greys began, and continued to c.1810.
1750	Yellow brick production started in London and continued to at least 1875. Header bond came into use about this time.
1770	Suffolk whites production began. Continued to c.1850.
1776	An Act passed to regulate brick sizes to 8½" x 4" x 2½".
1780	Norfolk whites production began. Continued to c.1860. Flemish stretcher bond noted from this time in the north-east. Dearne's bond came into use in the late eighteenth century.
1784	The Brick Tax began. Brick thicknesses tended to increase to three inches.

c.1820	Beginning of mechanised brick-making.
c.1831	The manufacture of 'heavy-pressed' bricks began. Rat-trap bond came into use about this time.
c.1850	'Wire-cut' bricks were first manufactured. English bond regained favour for Gothic revival and structural work.
1870	The production of Ruabon and Accrington bloods began. Popular for forty years. Multi-coloured brickwork fashionable for smaller buildings. In vogue for forty years.
c.1900 south-east.	Large scale production of yellow bricks began in the

Bibliography

1. M.W. Barley, The English Farmhouse and Cottage, 1961.
2. R.W. Brunskill, Brick Building in Britain, 1990.
3. A. Clifton-Taylor, The Pattern of English Building, 1965.
4. G. Darley, Built in Britain, 1983.
5. E. Gray, The British House, 1994.
6. D. Iredale and J. Barrett, Discovering Your Old House, 1991.
7. N. Lloyd, A History of English Brickwork, 1983.
8. E. Mercer, English Vernacular Houses, 1975.
9. Moxon, Mechanick Exercises or the Doctrine of Handy-Works, 1677.
10. S. Muthesius, The English Terraced House, 1982.
11. R. Neve, The City and Country Purchaser and Builders Dictionary, 2nd Edition, 1726.
12. M. Saunders, The Historic Home Owners Companion, 1987.
13. J. Woodforde, Bricks to Build a House, 1976.
14. Personal communication from R.M. Higgins Associates.
15. A. Brian, Vernacular Architecture, Vol.11, 1980.
16. J. Blair and N. Ramsey, English Medieval Industries, 1991.
17. T.P. Smith, The Medieval Brickmaking Industry in England, 1400-1450 (BAR British Series 138), 1985.

CHIMNEYS

Chimneys were in use from Norman times in important buildings such as castles, abbeys and first floor halls, but in lowlier dwellings, with central hearths, smoke leaked through the roof, sometimes aided by a louvre or gablet in the gable end; smoke hoods and smoke bays were later developments, constructed of timber. Here we are concerned with the chimneys visible from the outside of a building. Coal became available in towns for domestic use during the fourteenth century, resulting in a rapid increase in chimney building, often in brick. An early record mentions a London chimney in 1308, and town chimneys were commonplace by 1500 (1). Brick chimneys were built in the smaller houses of the countryside in the early sixteenth century, eliminating smoke, and permitting the insertion of an extra floor in hall houses; Wales tended to lag English developments by fifty years (1). For several centuries, chimneys were important status symbols, and much care was lavished on their embellishment, giving stylistic changes which provide a useful dating tool.

Fig 1.

Plain, cylindrical chimneys were usual in the Norman period, and until the early thirteenth century, and the Boothby Pagnell manor house c.1200 and the Jew's House at Lincoln c.1175 are two well-known examples. This shape was still in use c.1280, when Aydon Castle in Northumberland (Fig.1) was built, but there it was improved by the addition of a conical rain cover, and lancet smoke vents. As befitted such an important status symbol, it appeared prominently on an outside wall. The vertical smoke vents are a feature which was used from the thirteenth to the early fifteenth centuries, as shown in Fig.2 (Abingdon Abbey c.1250) and Figs.4 to 6.

After some experimentation with rectangular designs, such as Abingdon Abbey and Westdean Rectory in East Sussex (Fig.3), chimneys tended to have hexagonal or octagonal cross-sections embellished with ecclesiastical details, such as trefoil-headed vents, gablets and the lancet apertures noted at Aydon. These styles persisted from the late thirteenth century into the early fifteenth.

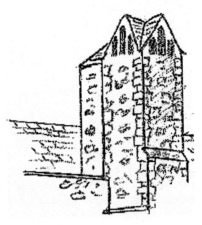

Fig 2.

Fig.4 is from Old Woodstock, Oxon, c.1290, and Fig.6 shows a monumental construction from Preston Plucknett in Somerset (early 15C).

Fig.5 shows a chimney from Grosmont Castle in Monmouthshire (14C), which has, in addition to trefoils and gablets, a set of spikes projecting from the top.

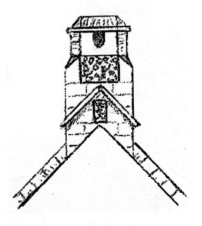

This feature appears to persist from the fourteenth century to the sixteenth century (Fig.7 15C, Fig.8

Fig 3.

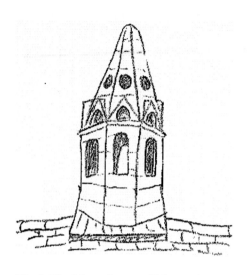

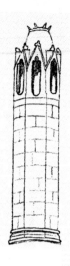

Fig 4. The Manor house, Old Woodstock,
Oxon. 1290

Fig 5. Grosmont Castle,
Monmouthshire.

Fig 6.

Abbey Farm,
Preston
Plucknett,
Somerset.

Early 15C

early 16C, Fig.9 late 16C); the spiral chimney in Fig.8 shows this form at its most highly developed. This star-topped shape may have been designed to break up turbulence at the chimney top, giving a smoother air flow, but this is pure conjecture!

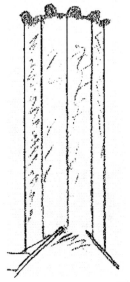

Fig 7.

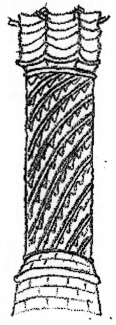

Fig 8.

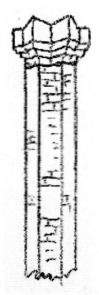

Fig 9.

The reign of Henry VIII, in the first half of the sixteenth century, was a period of lavish display, and beautiful chimney shafts built from carefully moulded bricks or terracotta rose on most houses of importance. Thornbury Castle in Gloucestershire (c.1514) shows many examples, and Figs.10 and 11 are from East Barsham Manor in Norfolk (c.1530).

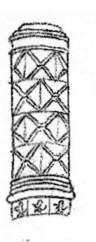 

By the middle of the sixteenth century, in the reign of Elizabeth, the fashion for decorated shafts was exhausted, and more classical forms, tending to look like columns with capitals, were the aim. The columns were smooth or fluted cylinders, or they retained the octagonal or hexagonal cross-section (Figs. 9, 12 & 13). Substantial bases, and the over-sailing brick courses at the top, were retained with many chimneys, as stylistic changes are usually gradual, and rarely drop all earlier features immediately.

Fig 12 (Left). Montacute House Somerset. Late 16C

Fig 13 (Right). Kirby Hall, Northants. c1572-1600

Fig.14 shows an extravagant example of this style from Chipping Campden (1620) displaying features typical of the Jacobean period such as strapwork on the base, a finial form for the top, and spiral fluting.

With the increase in the use of chimneys, a single house could have several separate chimneys, and as early as 1550 a house in London had four flues grouped in one stack (1). The problem of grouping chimneys into a stable and aesthetically pleasing composition prompted several different styles of chimney stack, which developed in parallel, until the simple rectangular brick stack of the early Georgian period was evolved. Stacks of square cross-section were often linked at their rims, and set diagonally to the face of the wall and to the axis of the roof; Fig.15 shows an example from Barnham Court in Sussex c.1640 and Fig.16 shows an earlier style from Gainsborough Old Hall, c.1600, where the hexagonal cross-section

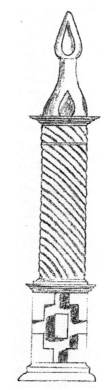

Fig 14. The Manor House Chipping Camden. Early 17C

was still in use. The diagonal fashion lasted from 1590 to 1690 (1), but was observed mainly in the first half of the seventeenth century. Fig.17 shows another form which lasted from the late sixteenth century to c.1650; square shafts were grouped together into a symmetrically disposed composition.

In areas where stone was used instead of brick, especially in the larger houses, the grouping of stacks in rows was used to produce an architectural composition.

The Talbot Inn in Oundle (1625) had four stacks grouped in a square with a flat entablature to unify the group (Fig.18).

Fig 15 (Left).

Fig 16 (Below)

Fig 17 (Above). Tenterden, Kent

Fig 18 (Right).

29

Fig.19 shows a row of chimneys at Bourne in Lincolnshire (c.1625), again linked by a common entablature, and a similar theme is shown in Fig.20 from Northamptonshire, dated 1658.

Fig.21, from Wansford in Cambridgeshire (1632), uses rustication to emphasise the massive nature of the group, but it also displays the feature of a recessed panel. These recesses were often arched - a typical Jacobean motif - and they served to lighten the design. Fig.22 shows a Kentish chimney (c.1714) still showing the recessed feature in a brick chimney stack. In some areas of the north this feature continued in use to 1750 (1). By the early part of the eighteenth century, stacks consisted of a plain rectangular mass of brickwork, with a single projecting course near the top (Fig.23). Even this detail was omitted towards the end of the eighteenth century.

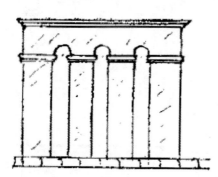

Fig 19. The Red Hall,
Bourne, Lincs. c1625

Fig 20.
Cotterstock Hall,
Northants. 1658

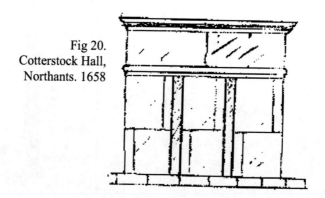

Fig 21. The Haycock Inn,
Wansford, Cambs. 1632

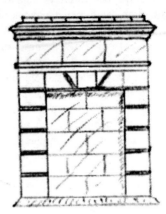

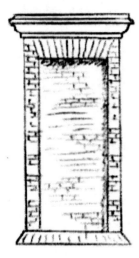

Fig 22. Bradbourne, Larkfield,
Kent. Early 18C

Fig 23.

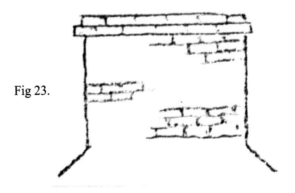

Early vernacular chimneys tended to be more concerned with ease of construction, and robust weatherproofing, rather than looking at the question of style. Fig.24 shows a stack on the Old Post Office at Tintagel, which dates from at least the early fifteenth century. The stack, which may be a later addition, has projecting ledges of stone to divert rain from the weak junction between the chimney stack and the roof. Fig.25 is from Townend House, Troutbeck (1623), and Fig.26 is from Coniston Old Hall (16C); both have the tapering cylinder form which is adopted when building with cobbles, which made it very difficult to produce a sharp corner. These also have drip ledges to deflect rainwater. In brick areas, chimney stacks for vernacular houses followed the developments shown in Figs.15, 17 and 23.

Nineteenth century chimney stacks tended to be heavy, unadorned, rectangular masses built with ashlar masonry or brick. However, when a revivalist effect was the aim, chimney stacks received much attention, and some interesting juxtapositions occurred. Prospect House in Hexham was re-vamped c.1895, and Flemish gables typical of the late seventeenth century were combined with an early sixteenth century chimney style (Fig.8) with spikes radiating profusely from the tall cylindrical chimney. Towards the end of the century, yellow brick stacks became a very common feature.

Bibliography

1.   E. Gray, The British House, 1994.

Other books containing useful information concerning chimneys, listed in order of importance:-

N. Lloyd, A History of the English House, 1931.
A. Quiney, The Traditional Buildings of England, 1990.
R.W. Brunskill, Brick Building in Britain, 1990.
V. Fletcher, Chimney Pots and Stacks, 1968.
M. Wood, The English Mediaeval House, 1965.

Fig 24.

Fig 25.

Fig 26.

33

DOORS

No systematic attempt is made in this section to differentiate between internal and external doors, as both were similarly constructed; the main difference was the more robust treatment required to enable an outer door to resist intruders. Many early doors consisted of three or more broad, vertical planks joined at their backs by horizontal planks called ledges (Fig.1). The Stillingfleet Viking hinge, illustrated in Fig.1 (Hinges chapter), was mounted on such a door, where the ledges were made from the split halves of a tree branch, showing this construction to have been in use as early as 1175. The nails which joined the front planks to the ledges were bent over (clenched) at the rear for security. Planks of roughly equal widths were used, but later doors sometimes chose to use a narrow central plank, flanked by two much wider planks in a symmetrical array. The

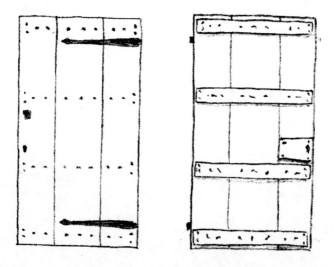

Fig 1. Front (Left), and rear.

ledged plank door has continued in use, albeit in unimportant locations, to the present day, with the addition of diagonal braces between the ledges to compensate for the thinner planks now in use.

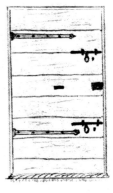

Fig 2. Front Above), and rear.

On doors which required extra strength, the ledges at the rear would be replaced by a complete back made of horizontal, clenched planks, as in Fig.2, which illustrates a Hexham door (c.1700) mounted at the entrance of an elegant five-bay house. This simple door proved unacceptable for the status of the house, as it was disguised in the late eighteenth century by the application of mouldings to produce a Georgian six-panel door. This desire to conceal the basic plank construction of the ledged plank door was always present in polite buildings, and Fig.3 shows the door of a fifteenth century house in Lavenham where mouldings have been applied to produce pointed tracery characteristic of that period. Where possible, the mouldings provided the added benefit of weatherproofing the joints between the planks.

Fig 3.

Fig.4 shows a sixteenth century door where joints are covered by heavy mouldings, and the panels are filled with linenfold decorative carving, which was a normal decoration for wall panels at that time. During most of the seventeenth century, the creased door, illustrated from Harvington Hall (c.1606; Fig.5) provided a simple method of decorating a plain door surface while providing draught-proofing. The neat, overlapping moulding emphasised the joins between planks by a light line of shadow. This technique was used even for small cupboard doors, and at the lowest vernacular levels; it possibly arose from the desire to use narrower planks, as wood supplies became less readily available.

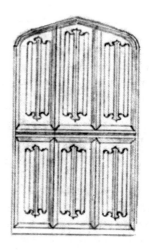

Fig 4.

Doors with simple rectangular panels are known from the late fifteenth century, at least. Fig.6 illustrates a mid-seventeenth century door of a type known from before 1500, where simple, unmoulded, narrow strips joined three broad planks together to give nine simple panels; these are embellished with quadrant or ogee mouldings in the angles. The strap hinges trapped between the wood surfaces were a standard method of fixing.

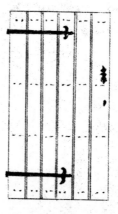

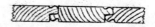

There was much experimentation in the seventeenth century in the design of panelled doors; whether this resulted from shortages in the

Fig 5.

supply of oak or the increasing availability of imported softwoods in large sizes is not clear. Fig.7 illustrates typical Jacobean and late Elizabethan motifs, used to decorate panels in the early seventeenth century. Fig.8 shows a polite eighteen-panel door (c.1606) which made use of quite small wood sections. Fig.9 is from later in the century when there was a tendency to use fewer panels. Plain eight-panel doors continued to be acceptable until c.1730 (2), and they occurred sporadically afterwards, but

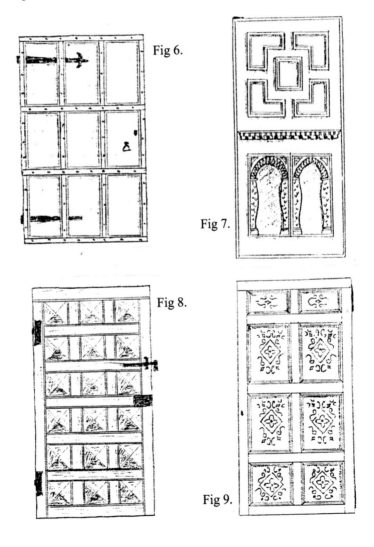

Fig 6.

Fig 7.

Fig 8.

Fig 9.

at no time do the proportions of the panels appear to have been standardised; Fig.17 (Doorways) shows one of the many alternatives.

Ten-panel doors are not illustrated, but these were used from the late seventeenth century to c.1730 (2), with various configurations.

The two-panel door illustrated in Fig.18 (Doorways) was used between c.1680 and 1740. A less frequently noted variant had three panels, with the centre panel smaller than those above and below, which were usually equal in size. Both door types used large bolection mouldings to frame the panels, similar to those used on wall panelling at that time. These doors used thin panels and were specifically for interior use.

An interesting, but short-lived, panel fashion used the St. Andrew's Cross (Fig.10). This type of door has been seen in London and Cambridge, on buildings dating from c.1730. It would be interesting to know whether these were intended as a sign of sympathy for the Jacobite cause which was to erupt fifteen years later.

By 1725, the six-panel door was becoming the generally accepted pattern for the Georgian house,

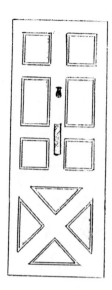

Fig 10. London, Early 18C

Fig 11. Hexham, 1780

38

and it continued in use until 1830 (2), re-occurring at intervals up to the late Victorian period. The panels were fielded, which meant that they were raised in their centres to a level which was flush with the surface of the door. Early examples sometimes fielded the top four panels only; in this case, the bottom panels were surrounded by a bead moulding, and were flush with the door surface (Fig.22 (Doorways)). This style gave more rain protection at the vulnerable lower part of the door. Up to c.1770 the tendency was to make the four lower panels equal in size, and larger than the upper two panels (Fig.27 (Doorways)), but c.1760 the pattern changed to that shown in Fig.11.

The Regency was a time of renewed experimentation with door panelling, probably as a reaction against the relative uniformity of the long Georgian phase. Fig.20 (Doorways) illustrates a six-panel door where four panels have been replaced with margined glazing such as was being used in

Fog 12.   Fig 13.

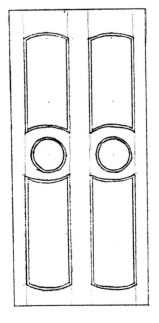 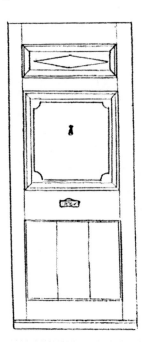

windows at that time. Fig.32 (Doorways) shows panels with motifs characteristic of the work of Sir John Soane, and Figs.12 and 13 show other Regency styles. Six equal panels were sometimes arranged in two horizontal rows of three, about this time, in the search for variety. Fig.14 shows a heavily-studded type which was popular c.1830; in some examples the two thin panels occupied nearly the whole length of the door. The heavy studding was possibly a precursor of the Gothic revival, and is reminiscent of Fig.12 (Doorways) where the door is probably a Regency replacement rather than an original. About 1830, the four-panel door came into general use, and it was the most common type until c.1890 (2). At this time stained or etched glass panels were being introduced into doors.

The reading of this chapter should be supplemented by reference to Alcock and Hall (1), which is an indispensable visual reference, illustrating many doors from the late sixteenth to the middle eighteenth

Fig 14.   Fig 15.
                                 C1830 & later.

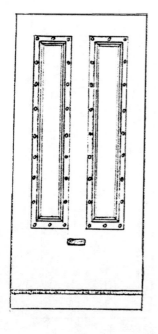
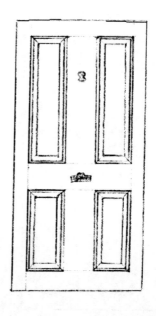

40

century. In addition, Lander (3) contains photographs of dated doors from the fifteenth to the late nineteenth century, and Gray (2) provides a dating glossary for doors (as for many other features), which covers doors in the period from c.1600 to the present.

Bibliography

1. N.W. Alcock and L. Hall, Fixtures and Fittings in Dated Houses (1567-1763), 1994.
2. E. Gray, The British House, 1994.
3. H. Lander, House and Cottage Interiors, 1982.
4. N. Lloyd, A History of the English House, 1931.
5. J. & M. Miller, Period details, 1993.

15C

DOORWAYS

Whenever money was available to embellish a house during its construction, attention was most frequently paid to the doorway, this being the prominent feature through which all important visitors must enter. This means that, particularly from the seventeenth century onwards, changes in fashionable details provided clues for the dating of doorways. Doorways, as opposed to doors, are specifically dealt with in this chapter, as they are relatively permanent features. Doors could easily be replaced after damage, and the temptation was to use the current fashion, if only because this was what was readily available. Conversely, because joinery was expensive, older doors are sometimes found re-used in newer doorways. Doors have been examined in the previous chapter.

Dates and initials found on a door lintel can normally be taken to show that the building is at least as old as the date shown, but the inscription may be celebrating a wedding rather than the date of construction. Another snag is that doorways were sometimes added on to a house, when money became available, some years after the date of erection. Tell-tale signs are metal straps tying the stonework into the main body of the house, and stone frames butting against a wall without being keyed in. The doorway is only one part of the investigation, and if a dated lintel or fashionable details are to be taken at face value, other features such as windows and chimneys should be of concordant styles. The illustrations show doorways from the twelfth to the early nineteenth century. After that time the eclectic tastes of the Victorians led to the adoption of a welter of styles from past history, and dating is more easily achieved from other features such as decorated brickwork or stylistic frills added to window lintels, which combine together to give the spirit of the age. A point to note in all studies of stylistic details is that doorways and other features are progressively adopted down the social scale thus extending the time range in which they were used. This is particularly applicable to the examples in this chapter which extend into the nineteenth century. When an illustration introduces a new dating feature, it is discussed in the notes accompanying that illustration rather than using an un-illustrated glossary.

Notes to Accompany Illustrations

1. (12C.) The Jew's House, Lincoln, c.1150.

Norman round-headed arch, with rich interlace decoration. Margaret Wood (12) should be consulted for full details of mediaeval doorways.

2. (12C.) Castle Hedingham, Essex, c.1130.

Semi-circular Norman doorhead decorated with characteristic chevron mouldings. (The door is 14C or later.)

3. (12C.) Boothby Pagnell Manor House, c.1180.

Early English. The head of the doorway is described as a corbelled lintel or square-headed trefoil (12). Simple doorways generally had chamfered jambs.

4. (13C to 15C.) Aydon Castle and Hexham Abbey, Northumberland, c. 1300.

The head of the doorway is described as a shouldered lintel or Caernarvon Arch from its use in Caernarvon castle. This style appeared initially in major buildings, but was mainly used in vernacular buildings towards the end of its period, especially in Devon.

5. (Early 13C to early 15C.)

The pointed, two-centred arch was the distinguishing feature of the change from the Romanesque (Norman period) to the Gothic (Early English and later) period. A drip-mould often followed the curve of the arch to throw rain off from important doorways. Jambs were usually chamfered. Towards the end of the fourteenth century the arch was often placed in a rectangular frame (12). R.W. Brunskill (2) gives details of the moulded profiles of drip-moulds and labels characteristic of doors from the fourteenth to the seventeenth century.

6. (Mainly 14C. Sporadically later to 17C (5).)

The ogee-headed arch has a convex curve in the lower part, going smoothly into a concave curve in the upper part. It was typical of the Decorated style which followed Early English. It was less commonly used than the two-centred arch.

Fig 4.

Fig 3.

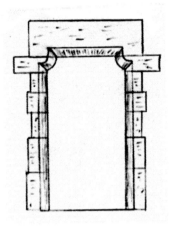

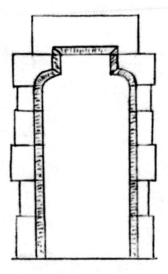

Fig 5.

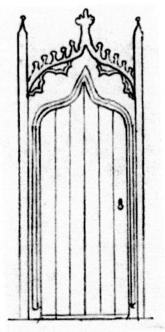

Fig 6.

7. (Late 14C to early 17C.) Church Street, Tewkesbury.

The depressed ogee arch was common in timber construction, but a stone example from the early seventeenth century is shown in Mercer's work (7). This illustrates the conservatism common to Yorkshire and the north-west of England.

8. (Early 14C to 17C.)

8a. Old Soar, Plaxtol, Kent. Early 14C.

8b. Bastle door, Allendale, Northumberland c. 1600.

The simple pointed arch with a bevelled edge to the arch and jambs was a long-lived vernacular form.

9. (Late 14C to end of 16C.)

If a broad doorway was constructed with a two-centred arch, it tended to rise to an inconvenient height. The solution was provided by the four-centred arch which combined four curves to provide a wide, elegant arch of convenient height. The triangular spandrels between the door frame and the rectangular surround were used for heraldic or decorative carving. A label mould was used above the doorway to deflect rainwater.

10. (15C to 17C.)

The Tudor arch was like a four-centred arch with flattened top sections. This process of simplification led to the false four-centred arch of the seventeenth century shown in illustration fifteen.

Fig 7.

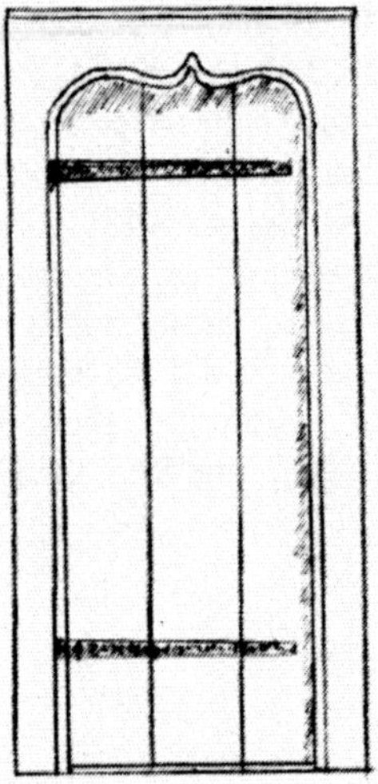

Fig 8a

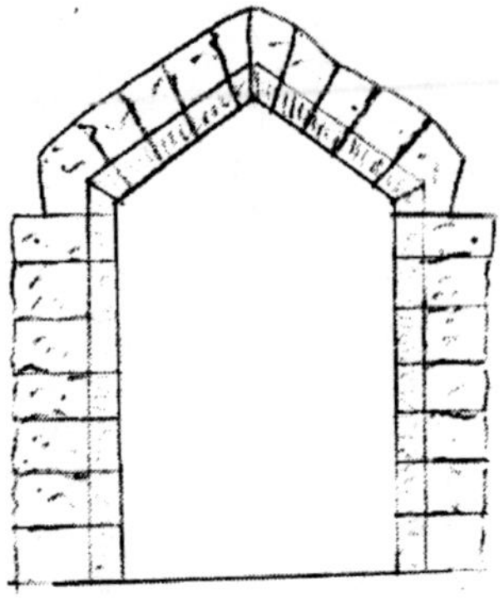

Fig 8b.

Fig 9.

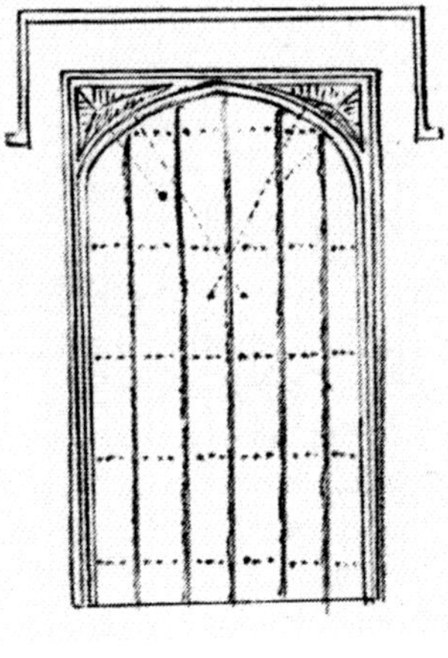

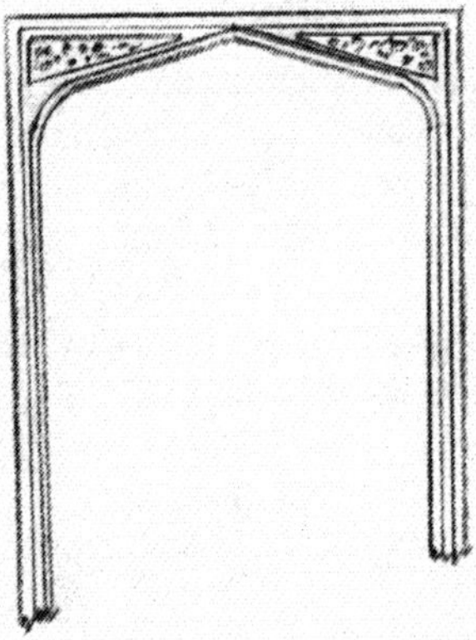

Fig 10.

11. (Late 16C to mid-19C.)

Round-headed doorways, which had been uncommon since Norman times, came back into use in highly ornate Elizabethan and Jacobean entries of the late sixteenth and early seventeenth centuries. At the vernacular level, round-headed doorways were cut from massive lintels to be seen in bastles from the early seventeenth century near Hexham. More sophisticated examples occur in this area at Ovingham (1697) and Hexham (c. 1700), and the form recurs at intervals into the nineteenth century when it was common in terraced housing. The earlier doorways were sometimes graced with flanking columns and semi-circular label moulds. Keystones at the top of the arch were an option throughout the period, appearing as sculpted heads made from Coade stone from the late eighteenth century.

12. Bourne Mill, Essex, 1591.

This shows the flamboyance of the early round-headed doorways. The roundheaded flutings on the pilasters are typical of the early seventeenth century; the fashion recurred nearly two hundred years later. The studded door is probably a Regency renovation (c. 1820).

13. (17C onwards.) Kirkoswald, Cumbria, 1622.

The rectangular door surround occurred in simple contexts in the Mediaeval period, but became commonplace from the seventeenth century. The example shows how considerable refinement could be conferred on a crude stone surround by a well cut roll-moulding in conjunction with a carved lintel. Illustrations 13a et seq. show a series of dated mouldings from seventeenth and eighteenth century door surrounds in Northumberland. The styles change at roughly twenty year intervals, giving a useful dating tool for this area. Similar sequences could be developed for other areas.

Fig 11.

Fig 12.

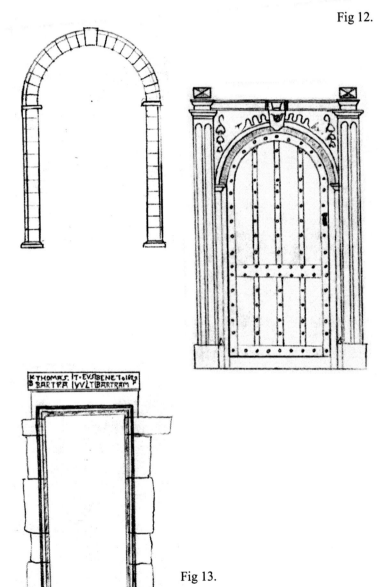

Fig 13.

13a. Shows two simple styles of the early seventeenth century. The roll-moulding had been in use for a long period and served to give distinction to an otherwise simple doorway. The bevelled door surround continued in use for simple doorways, until at least the end of the eighteenth century.

13b. Shows door surrounds from the middle of the seventeenth century.

They are distinguished by a series of fine, closely spaced mouldings, which combine to give a recessed aperture for the door.

13c. As the seventeenth century progressed there seems to have been a desire for simplification, characterised by the use of the ogee curve, and little other adornment in the later versions.

Fig 13c.
Simple.
Early 17C

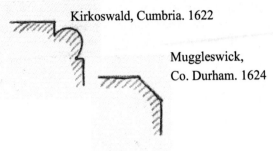

Kirkoswald, Cumbria. 1622

Muggleswick,
Co. Durham. 1624

Fig 13b.
Recessed/fluted.
c1640-1660

Fig 13c. Ogee Curves.
c1660-1690

Holy Island House,
Hexham. 1657

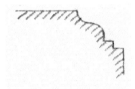

Simonburn Rectory,
Northumberland. 1660

Acomb, nr. Hexham
1657

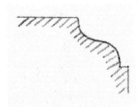

High Shield, Hexham.
c1683

Wall, nr. Hexham.
1642

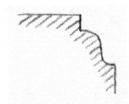

Priest's House, Hexham.
1688

13d. At the turn of the century, the influence of Wren was everywhere apparent, as a doorway with any pretensions whatsoever had to be embellished with a fat bolection moulding. It was a short-lived fashion, but of considerable value for dating purposes.

Fig 13d. Bolection Mouldings. c1680-1710

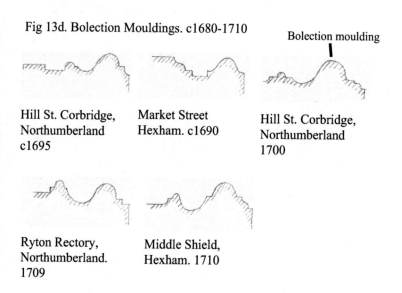

Bolection moulding

Hill St. Corbridge, Northumberland c1695

Market Street Hexham. c1690

Hill St. Corbridge, Northumberland 1700

Ryton Rectory, Northumberland. 1709

Middle Shield, Hexham. 1710

13e. The next common development was the use of two flat surfaces running round the jambs and lintel. This is referred to as the doubled-architrave. From a distance, the minor mouldings do not stand out, and the appearance is quite distinctive as two flat surfaces side-by-side, even in the example from Cumbria, where one surface is not flat but composed of a series of steps.

Fig 13e. Doubled-Architrave Mouldings. c1720-1740

St. Mary's Chare, Hexham. c1720

Middleham, Yorkshire. 1732

Hall Stile Bank, Hexham. c1736

Romaldskirk,
Yorkshire. 1733

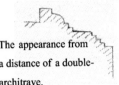

The appearance from
a distance of a double-
architrave.

Acorn House,
Cumbria. 1740

Barnard Castle,
Co. Durham. 1742

13f. The second half of the eighteenth century is characterised by very simple door surrounds. Likewise ironwork on doors assumed much simpler forms, joining in a trend to simplification dictated by economy or aesthetic preference?

Fig 13f. A return To Simple Surrounds. Post 1750

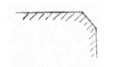

Acomb,
Northumberland.
1750

Greenhead,
Northumberland.
1752

High shield,
Hexham.
1770

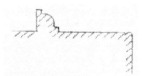

Melmerby,
Cumbria. 1789

Causeway House,
Vindolanda,
Northumberland. 1770

14. (Mid 17C to mid 18C.) Hawes, Wensleydale, 1668.

Inscribed doorways, topped by an oval-headed basket arch, carved from a massive lintel, are a characteristic northern form, noted as late as 1752 at Ryton in Northumberland. They derive from the four-centred arch, the continuous curve being simpler to cut. Splayed jambs were the usual form for these simple doorways.

15. (c.1625 to c.1725.) Newbiggin, Wensleydale, 1670.

The false four-centred arch was the final simplification of the shaped doorhead, before purely rectangular doorways became the norm. Examples can be observed in most of the northern counties of England.

16. (Early 17C to c. 1700.)

Carved, dated lintels, above rectangular doorways, are to be seen in Yorkshire, Cumbria and Northumberland. This fashion may have been earliest in Northumberland, moving elsewhere in the latter third of the seventeenth century. Bevelled doorjambs with stop-moulding towards the lower part of the jamb were combined with these lintels.

Fig 14.

Fig 15.

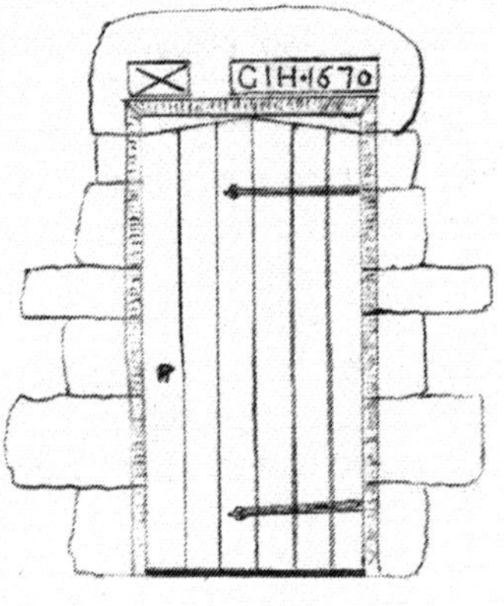

ANO DOM 1668
GOD BEING WITH VS
WHO CANBE AGAINST
THE

CIH·1670

Fig 16.

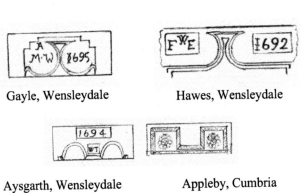

A
M·W 1695

Gayle, Wensleydale

F W E   1692

Hawes, Wensleydale

1694
WT

Aysgarth, Wensleydale

Appleby, Cumbria

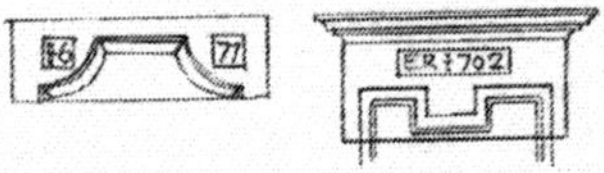

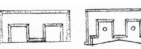

56   77

ER 1702

Decorated lintes from northern
stone districts, mainly
Pennines and Lake district.

Updated lintel
with drip
mould.
Hexham.
Early 17C

Updated lintel
with drip mould
& shouldered
moulding.
Hexham

17. (Mid 17C onwards.)

The top part of the illustration shows a segmental pediment, which is supported at each side by brackets to form a projecting rain shield over the door. Segmental pediments on doorways appeared from the middle of the seventeenth century, but were most common in London from 1680 to c.1720, and especially from 1700 to 1715 (3). In the north-east they occur somewhat later (e.g. Barnard Castle 1742, Greenhead 1757). The supporting brackets appeared from the middle of the seventeenth century to c.1730, and then sporadically into the nineteenth century. They were usually of wood and were often elaborately carved with acanthus leaves, cherubic heads and similar motifs. The 1707/9 Building Acts banned wooden details of this sort in London because of the fire hazard which they represented, and so their popularity gradually waned. A specialised form of bracket called a console is shown in illustration 24. The surround to the door frame, called the architrave, has a squared projection at the top on each side. This is referred to as a shouldered or lugged architrave; these occurred from c. 1625 to c.1775. In the north east, this feature was common in the second quarter of the eighteenth century.

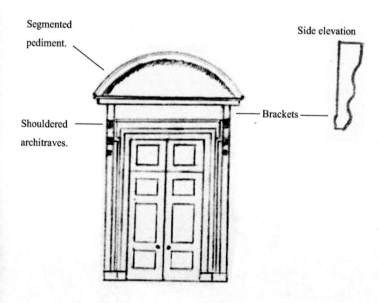

Segmented pediment.

Side elevation

Shouldered architraves.

Brackets

18. (Late 17C to early 18C.)
Market Street,
Hexham, c.1690.

The segmental pediment has a gap
in the middle and is called a split
or broken segmental pediment.
The open ends of the pediment
were normally terminated by a
rosette or scroll. In this case the
full description is split, scrolled
pediment.

Fig 18.

19. (c.1680 to early 18C.)

Projecting hoods, supported on brackets above a doorway, had a brief
popularity lasting for upwards of thirty years. Some were semi-elliptic, but
the majority take the semi-cylindrical form. Some early examples were
filled with carved flowers, fruit and other naturalistic motifs, and the
brackets were similarly ornamented. Later examples took the shell form or
combined this with the earlier decoration in a very elaborate display. The
Building Acts were probably responsible for the early demise of this
highly inflammable style.

Fig 19.

20. (Late 17C to early 18C.) Ryton, Northumberland, 1709.

Fig 20.

The main feature to note is the pediment, which may be described as a swan-necked, split, scrolled pediment. This style occurred from c.1660 to c.1720 (5) but tended to a narrower date span in any selected part of the country. Below the broken base of the pediment is a pulvinated frieze, bearing the inscription NON NOBIS. This frieze is convex and rounded at the ends, and is very typical of the second quarter of the eighteenth century. The door architrave incorporates a bolection moulding (see 13a et seq.). This was common in Northumberland from c.1680 to c.1710; it was noted as early as 1664 in Kent.

21. (Late 17C to c.1750, sporadically later.)

The cantilevered, hooded doorcase is supported by richly carved brackets; consoles were an alternative support (see 24). The Building Acts

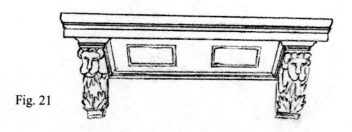

Fig. 21

legislated to ban these flammable wooden features, but with limited success.

22. (Late 17C to early 19C.) Middleham, Yorkshire, 1732.

The triangular pediment was used from the late seventeenth century and throughout the eighteenth. A split top indicates a date in the early eighteenth century. An opening in the bottom of the pediment, large enough to allow the semi-circular fanlight to fill the inside of the pediment, was fashionable from c.1750. The shouldered architrave and pulvinated frieze are described in illustrations 17 and 20. The use of small square blocks called dentils, to decorate the pediment, occurred from at least 1715 to the nineteenth century. They were particularly common in exterior work between 1730 and 1760 (5).

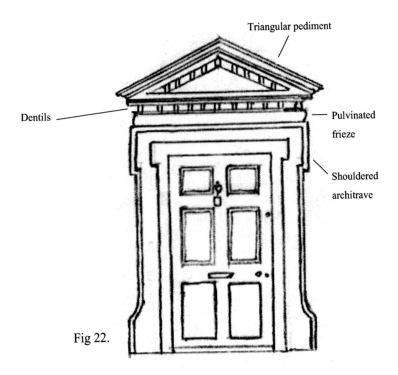

Triangular pediment

Dentils

Pulvinated frieze

Shouldered architrave

Fig 22.

23. (Late 17C to late 18C.)Greenhead, Northumberland, 1757.

The Corinthian columns were popularised by Wren in the Baroque period of the late seventeenth century, and their use continued to c.1720 in London (3), but much later in the provinces. The door is relatively modern.

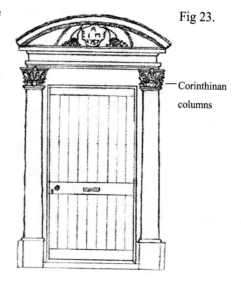

Fig 23.

Corinthinan columns

24. (Especially early 18C.)

The console is a bracket, normally S-shaped, which is taller than it is wide. It was used to support door hoods, and was popular to at least 1760, occurring sporadically later.

Fig 24.

Fig 25.

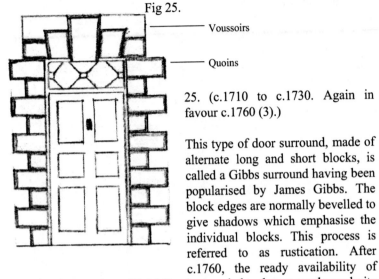

Voussoirs

Quoins

25. (c.1710 to c.1730. Again in favour c.1760 (3).)

This type of door surround, made of alternate long and short blocks, is called a Gibbs surround having been popularised by James Gibbs. The block edges are normally bevelled to give shadows which emphasise the individual blocks. This process is referred to as rustication. After c.1760, the ready availability of blocks made from the artificial Coade stone led to the renewed popularity of this style.

26. (c.1680 to 19C.)

· Fig 26.

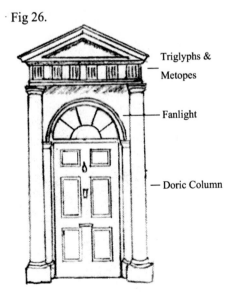

Triglyphs & Metopes

Fanlight

Doric Column

Doric columns were in use for a protracted period. Gray (5) indicates that the fluted Roman type flourished from 1680 to 1730. The usual process of cheapening by simplification, nowadays glibly referred to as value engineering, led to the use of unfluted columns (1730 to 1880 (5)). Greek styles followed from c.1810 to 1840. The frieze under the pediment contains plain sections called metopes and three-grooved sections called triglyphs. This style was in use by 1700, but flourished in the middle half of the eighteenth century in the provinces. The Adam brothers popularised more ornate friezes in the late eighteenth century. Fanlights are discussed in the chapter on windows.

27. (c.1750 to late 1800.) Woodbridge, Suffolk c.1770.

The decorative frieze and fluted Corinthian columns show the Adam influence typical of the later part of the eighteenth century.

Fig 27.

28. (c.1750 to c.1830.)

The semi-circular fanlight occupying the whole of an open triangular pediment (broken entablature) is the main feature to note. This arrangement was very commonly used in the last quarter of the eighteenth century. Arches with keystones occur from very early times and do not form a useful dating feature. However, Coade-stone versions, which were available from 1763 onwards, are readily recognised and can be of use for dating.

29. (18C and early 19C.)

The Ionic columns are characterised by flat capitals with scrolls at the corner. They were frequently associated with a pulvinated frieze and dentils. Not a useful dating system.

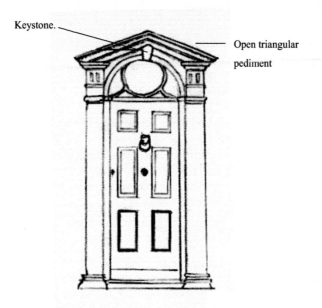

Keystone.

Open triangular pediment

Fig 28.

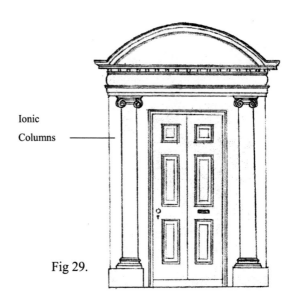

Ionic Columns

Fig 29.

30. (Late 18C.)

The decorated frieze is typical late eighteenth century in style, as is the partial disappearance of the fanlight.

31. (c.1770 into 19C.) Bedford Square, London.

This style is recognised by the rusticated, Coade-stone blocks, windows flanking the door and the large delicate fanlight. It occurs mainly in the last thirty years of the eighteenth century. Rustication is used here with its original meaning, which referred to the tooling on the block surfaces, meant to convey an impression of massive strength. The usage of rustication in illustration 25, was a later meaning.

32. (Late 18C to early 19C.)

The semi-circular top to the door surround, combined with the moulded surround and the roundels on either side, are typical of Regency doorways. Reeded pilasters and rosettes in place of the roundels were also characteristic for this period. The highly ornate door panelling was an attempt to get away from the rigidity imposed by the six-panel Georgian door for nearly a century.

Bibliography

1.   M.S. Briggs, Everyman's Concise Encyclopaedia of Architecture, 1966.
2.   R.W. Brunskill, Illustrated Handbook of Vernacular Architecture, 1971. (Mouldings.)
3.   D. Cruickshank and P. Wyld, Georgian Town Houses and their Details, 1990. (Dated details.)
4.   P. Cunnington, How Old is Your House? 1980.
5.   E. Gray, The British House, 1994. (Dating.)
6.   N. Lloyd, A History of the English House, 1931. (Dated illustrations.)
7.   E. Mercer, English Vernacular Houses, 1975.
8.   Northern Heritage Consultancy Ltd., Townscape, 1990. (Wide date range.)
9.   J. Penoyre and M. Ryan, The Observer's Book of Architecture, 1963.
10.   A. Quiney, Period Houses, 1989.

11. RCOHM, York: Historic Buildings in the Central Area, 1981.
12. M. Wood, The English Mediaeval House, 1965.
   (Mediaeval detail).

Fig 30.

Fig 31.

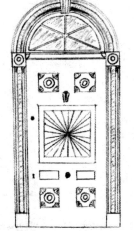

Fig 32.

FIREPLACES

Open hearths were the usual method of heating small dwellings until the sixteenth century, but fireplaces with chimneys or hoods were used in important buildings from early times. Once a particular type became established, it tended to persist for a very long period, and it is only by noting specific stylistic details that an attempt at dating can be made.

The first figure shows a fireplace in Colchester Keep (c.1090). The rough semi-circular arch, which is typical early Norman work, made use of the copious supplies of bricks from the old Roman defences. The herring-bone pattern in the back of the fireplace is a recurring feature up to the seventeenth century. The semi-circular arch is a special case of the segmented arch shown in Fig.2 from Rievaulx Abbey (c.1132); this was used in large kitchens until the end of the sixteenth century, and a small example occurred as late as 1765 in Berwick Town Hall. A later

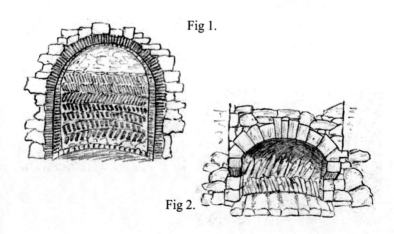

Fig 1.

Fig 2.

circular-headed Norman fireplace from Castle Hedingham (c.1140) is illustrated in Fig.3. Greater sophistication is shown, with columns and characteristic mouldings.

Corbels were preferred instead of columns by the end of the thirteenth century (12), although they were occasionally seen until the end of the fifteenth century. Columns again came into fashion about 1580 in Elizabethan and Jacobean fireplaces, persisting until the end of the seventeenth century (4).

Fig 3.

Hooded fireplaces came into use towards the end of the twelfth century (12). The example in Fig.4 is from Boothby Pagnell (c.1200). The type persisted to the early fourteenth century, and again came into use with some decorative brick examples built in the sixteenth century. The Boothby Pagnell lintel is constructed from several pieces of stone jointed together by a process known as joggling.

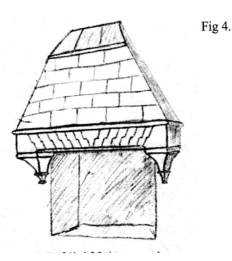

Fig 4.

By 1260, this process was reduced to joggling just at the ends of a massive lintel as shown in Fig.5 from Castle Bolton (c.1260) (12).

Fig 5.

In later examples, complete lintels spanned the whole width of the fireplace as in the local example from Aydon Castle (c.1280) in Fig.6. At the vernacular level, these grand examples were reduced to the simple form of Fig.7. This type was common in the fifteenth century and it persisted in the north into the late seventeenth century.

In the fourteenth century, hooded fireplaces were gradually replaced by fireplaces with a rectangular aperture built into the thickness of the wall. This basic shape has persisted to the present day, and dating relies on noting the details which embellish the edges of the aperture or the panel above the aperture. Fig.8 is an example from McClellan's Tower in Kirkcudbright (c.1582), where a pronounced roll-moulding decorates the edge of the opening. This simple but very effective treatment was in use from the beginning of the sixteenth century, or earlier, until well into the seventeenth century (4).

In Northumberland, the roll moulding can be seen on some of the more sophisticated bastle doors of the early seventeenth century, illustrating the frequently noted parallels between doorway and fireplace apertures.

Fig 6.

Fig 7.

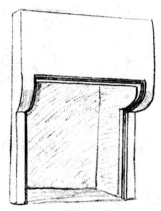

Fig 8.

Fig.9 shows a simple rectangular vernacular hearth common from the sixteenth century up to the end of the seventeenth century; a plain chamfer surrounds the whole of the aperture. Timber-framed houses of the south-east substituted a massive oak lintel for the stone lintel of the north, to give the very wide type illustrated in Fig.10. Proper chimneys, built with brick, provided safe fireplaces for timber houses from the early sixteenth century, and g seats, herringbone brickwork and aumbries for dry storage of salt were typical features.

At the upper end of the social scale more sophistication was desired, and Fig.11 from the Abbot's Parlour at Muchelney (c.1508) shows the decorative use of quatrefoil panels above the fireplace. Quatrefoils were a popular motif in the last forty years of the fifteenth century, remaining in vogue well into the sixteenth century (12). The moulding around the aperture is stopped one third of the way up from the bottom in a manner typical of the second half of the sixteenth and the early seventeenth centuries (6). This feature was seen occasionally in the fifteenth century (12). A third feature of this particular fireplace is the cornice and the flanking columns, which had a brief vogue from the middle to the end of the fifteenth century.

The four-centred arch came into use in the fourteenth century as a decorative method for spanning rectangular fireplace apertures. Fig.12 illustrates this type, which was in use from the late fourteenth until the seventeenth century (4). By the middle of the fifteenth century the debased four-centred arch came into use, in parallel with the true arch. This was

Fig 9.

70

Fig 10.

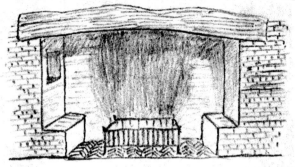

Fig 11.

Fig 12.

typical of the ever-present trend to attempt to reduce the work involved in making elaborate ornament. In this case, the work of making the four separate curved elements, which made up the four-centred arch, was reduced by making two long straight sections for the top of the arch as illustrated in Fig.13, which shows a typically lavish Jacobean example from Bessie Surtees House in Newcastle. Towards the end of the fifteenth century, a further simplification was provided by the cambered head type illustrated in Fig.14 by an example, probably of seventeenth century date, from Allensford in Northumberland. In this example, the spandrels are slightly recessed for decorative effect. Note that the simple chamfer of the jambs is stopped quite close to the base, unlike the examples noted from an earlier period in the south. The cambered arch continued in use for doorways in Northumberland and Yorkshire until the early eighteenth century, and it is probable that cambered fireplaces continued until then.

Fig 13.

Fig 14.

Stylistic features for doorways and fireplaces of the late seventeenth and eighteenth centuries were often similar. Fig.15 shows a fireplace surround with a pronounced bolection moulding, very similar to that used on doorways in the period c.1660 to 1730. In Northumberland, this style appears mainly between c.1680 and 1710. It must again be emphasised that, with most dating features, it is necessary to study the time-span for a feature in a particular locality, by noting dated examples. Time lags of twenty or thirty years between the adoption of a feature in different parts of England were probably common, but lags of up to one hundred years have only generally been noted for the north-west of England where there were possibly conservative elements who preferred to stick to older styles from choice rather than from ignorance.

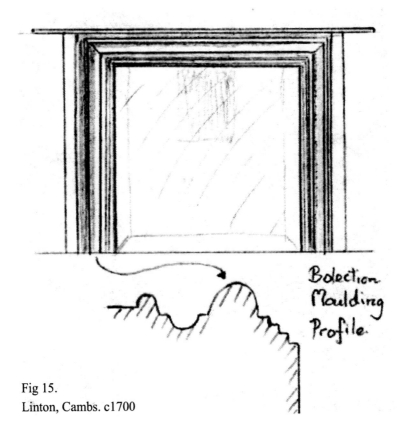

Bolection
Moulding
Profile.

Fig 15.
Linton, Cambs. c1700

Some early eighteenth century fireplaces, c.1710 to 1740, featured flat, single or double architraves (cf. Doorways Fig.13e) with shoulders or lugs at the corners (Fig.16). A desire for greater elaboration led to the use of pulvinated friezes, with centre panels, and inverted scrolls (Fig.17) in the period c.1725 to 1765. With the influence of Adam, dominating decoration between 1765 and 1800, restrained elegance was in favour (Fig.18), and there was much experimentation with Etruscan, Gothic and Chinoiserie decoration. Coloured stoneware tablets and medallions were mass-produced and set into wood or marble surrounds. In the early nineteenth century, the Greek revival led to the use of key patterns, pilasters and triangular pediments for fireplace ornamentation. The final illustration (Fig.19) shows a typical simple Regency style of the early nineteenth century, with roundels or floral motifs in the corners, and sometimes in the centre panel, together with fluted pilasters flanking the sides. Detail in the late eighteenth century and throughout the nineteenth century was such that accurate dating becomes progressively more difficult, and the best recourse for this period is to study one of the illustrated volumes mentioned in the bibliography.

Bibliography

1. O. Cook, The English House through Seven Centuries, 1984.
2. D.J. Eveleigh, Firegrates and Kitchen Ranges, (Shire).
3. H. Forrester, The Smaller Queen Anne and Georgian House, 1700 to 1840, 1964.
4. E. Gray, The British House, 1994.
5. A. Kelly, The Book of English Fireplaces, 1968.
6. H. Lander, House and Cottage Interiors, 1982. (Illustrations.)
7. N. Lloyd, A History of the English House, 1931.
8. E.V.H. Mercer, English Vernacular Houses, 1975.
9. J. Miller, Period Fireplaces, 1995. (Illustrations.)
10. J. and M. Miller, Period Details, 1993. (Illustrations.)
11. S.C. Ramsey and J.D.M. Harvey, Small Georgian Houses and their Details, 1750-1820, 1990.
12. M. Wood, The English Medieval House, 1981.

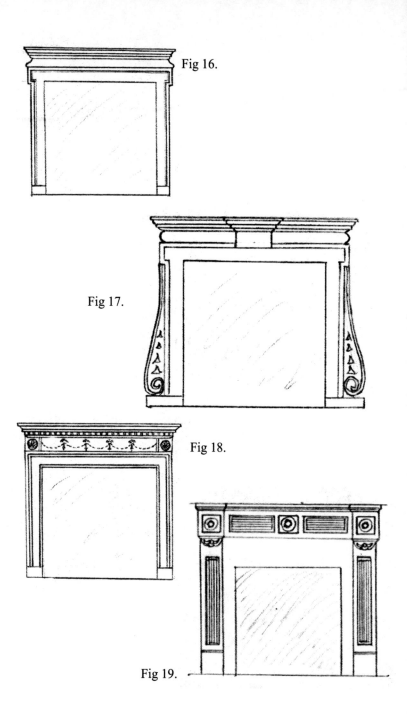

Fig 16.

Fig 17.

Fig 18.

Fig 19.

Brick crowsteps (Fig.2) on gable ends were popular in Norfolk, being an example of the continental influence on much of the earlier English brick-building, and they were common during the sixteenth century. The parapets of the North Bar at Beverley were finished with crowsteps in 1410 (7), and a gable example was noted as early as 1434 at Ewelme in Oxfordshire (2), and as late as 1698 at Thurton in Norfolk (5). Stone crow-steps became common in the Lake District in the eighteenth century (3). In the late sixteenth century, the same continental influences led to strapwork flourishes on gable ends exemplified by Figs.3 and 4. Strapwork was a prevalent decorative motif in the late Elizabethan and Jacobean periods; finials were also typically Jacobean, and were reputed to prevent the devil from sitting on the roof.

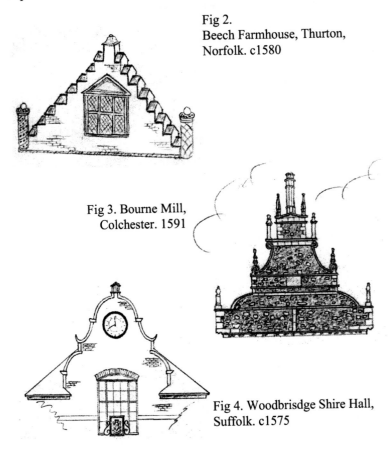

Fig 2.
Beech Farmhouse, Thurton, Norfolk. c1580

Fig 3. Bourne Mill, Colchester. 1591

Fig 4. Woodbrisdge Shire Hall, Suffolk. c1575

In the early seventeenth century, Flemish gables became fashionable, displaying combinations of curves and steps (Figs.5 and 6).

The first were probably seen in Norfolk in 1578, and in Kent c.1610, but they were particularly popular in the eastern counties between 1670 and 1720. They were re-introduced in the late Victorian period. Hexham, typically, has ten examples of Flemish or Dutch gables which were all built within the twenty years between 1880 and 1900, after which time no more were erected. They provide an excellent example of the volatility and short duration of many fashions in architecture.

A simpler style of gable with horizontal stepped endings to the gable coping was common in the first half of the seventeenth century (Fig.8). The steps were frequently adorned with decorative finials. In 1631, Kew Palace, in London, was built with the so-called Dutch gables (Fig.7) which differed from the Flemish type in having a classical pediment on the top. They have been noted on a building dating from 1618 (6), and they were popular from 1630 to 1650 and sporadically afterwards. Pevsner considered them to be a little out of date by 1675, but he noted them as continuing in use to 1736 in north-west Norfolk. Dated Kentish examples have been noted up to the late seventeenth century (1).

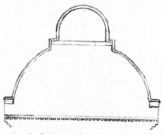

Fig 5. Huntingfield High House,
Suffolk. 1700

Fig 6.

a) Stud Farm, Stratford St. Andrew,
Suffolk. Late 17C.
b) Manor Farm, Sawtry, Cambs. 1672
c) Treasury Farm, Ickham, Kent. 1633
d) Pound Farm, Hevingham, Norfolk.
1675

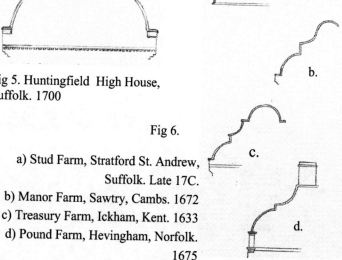

Fig 7.
Kew Palace, London. 1631

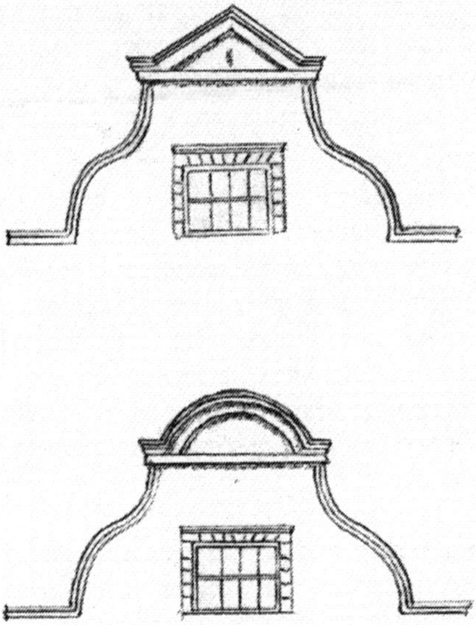

Fig 8.

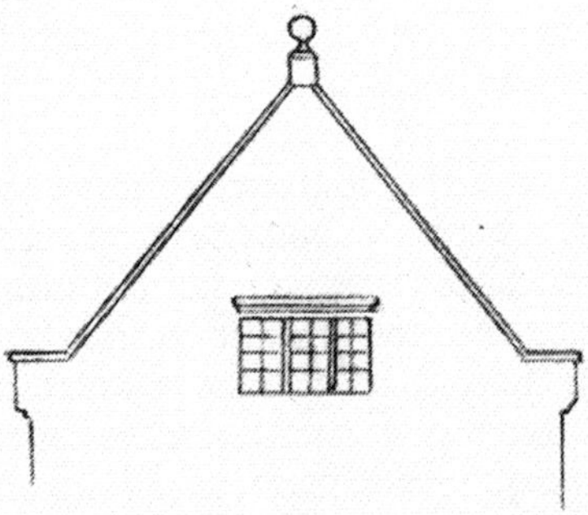

Bateman's, Burwash
Sussex. C1643

Corbridge,
Northumberland. 17C

Several vernacular methods were used during the seventeenth and eighteenth centuries to produce gables which were raised above the roof covering to protect the thatch, slates etc., from wind damage. Fig.9 shows inverted crowsteps; overlapping blocks of stone combine to form a narrow, water-resistant edging to the gable. This style is common in Northumberland, and occurs in stone districts as far south as Rutland. It is of restricted use for dating purposes, having been noted on buildings dating from c.1600 to c.1770 in Northumberland. Flat coping stones (Fig.10a), having the lowest stone pinned into the main body of masonry, can be observed on buildings dating from the fourteenth century. In some versions, the coping stones are stepped and lipped over each other to prevent water penetration at the junctions. Kneelers were adopted early in the seventeenth century to prevent coping stones from sliding down the gable edge. Figs.10b and 11 illustrate some of the various shapes of kneeler to be seen.

The earliest style with its steep cyma curve, and the ornate late Victorian styles, are the most useful for dating purposes. The intervening styles do not necessarily correspond to the date of erection of the building; they can equally indicate the period when the roof pitch was altered to take Welsh slates, or perhaps when the roof was raised; caution is essential. Kneelers were obsolete in the south after c.1750.

Brick on edge (Fig.10c) was a convenient method of providing a crisp gable edge, but it was prone to damp penetration as the mortar decayed. Dating of this style is very much a matter for local investigation and comparison. Another brick treatment was called tumbling or tumbling-in (Fig.12). This is decorative and provides an uncut brick edge to the gable, which resists frost damage and water penetration. It was common in East Anglia from the middle of the seventeenth century until the end of the eighteenth century. It remained in favour in some places into the nineteenth century, and is still seen on the occasional new building up to the present. This style penetrated Northumberland, as far west as Hexham, near the end of the seventeenth century. Tumbling remained in favour in eastern counties until the middle of the eighteenth century, at least, and is still occasionally used for vernacular revival work.

Fig 9.

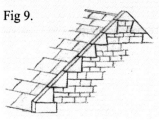

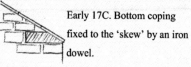

Fig 11. (After George Sheeran).

Early 17C. Bottom coping fixed to the 'skew' by an iron dowel.

C1620 & later. A 'kneeler' came into use. The profile was a steep cyma curve.

Fig 10a.

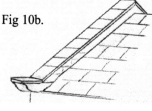

In the 18C kneelers became larger and showed a variety of curved profiles.

C1800, profiles were simplified to a shallow cyma curve.

Fig 10b.

Fig 10c.

Ornate mid to late Victorian. Corbridge, Northumberland.

'Scrolled skewputt.' a Scottish style to be seen in Berwick on Tweed and Rothbury, Northumberland. Often inscribed with a date. Also seen in Cumbria and Cornwall.

Fig 12.

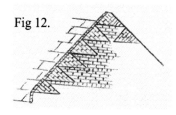

Bibliography

1. R.J. Brown, English Farmhouses, 1982.
2. A. Clifton-Taylor, The Pattern of English Building, 1965.
3. E. Gray, The British House, 1994.

4. D. Iredale and J. Barrett, Discovering Your Old House, 1991.
5. N. Pevsner, The Buildings of England: Northwest and South Norfolk, 1962.
6. N. Pevsner, The Buildings of England: Northeast Norfolk and Norwich, 1962.
7. T.P. Smith, The Medieval Brickmaking Industry in England, 1400-1450 (BAR British series 138), 1985.
8. G. Sheeran, Good Houses Built of Stone, 1986.

HINGES AND MISCELLANEOUS IRONWORK

Hinges

The high cost of joinery and blacksmith work has meant that, once a door hinge is nailed into position, the door may become one of the longest lasting features of a house. Hinges and the associated metalwork on a door were, until a recent publication by Alcock & Hall (1), an unpublicised method of dating houses, which is particularly useful for the period 1600 to 1750. Their book illustrates a wide range of metalwork from this period and it is an indispensable source. Here, the aim is to show further examples, in order to extend the date range, and to show something of the general interest that this subject holds, besides its use for dating.

Salzman (11) makes it clear that most of the general hinge types were in use from early medieval times; they were treated as important decorative objects, as well as being functional. Over the centuries there was a gradual change towards simplicity, until the early eighteenth century, when function became all important and plainer styles prevailed. There was a brief recrudescence of elaborate reproduction hinges in the Victorian Gothic period, and then a lapse until the reproduction work of the present day.

Hook-hinge refers to the type of hinge illustrated from Appleby Castle (Fig.10) where the end of the hinge is bent into a loop which dropped over a pivot-post fixed to the wall. Salzman (11) notes that the majority of doors from the late thirteenth century used hook hinges.

This name is to be preferred to strap hinge, which is a modern term normally used to refer to hinges of a type which was originally called a cross-garnet. The old term for the hook-hinge was probably a garnet, this term being used as late as 1726 by Neve (10). The Oxford English Dictionary suggests that garnet derives from Norman French carne or Latin cardinal, both meaning a hinge. The Stillingfleet hinge (Fig.1), with its Viking longboat, may possibly be a Viking display of smithing virtuosity re-used in 1145.

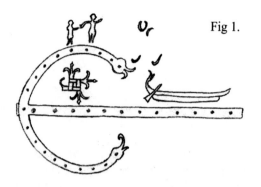

Fig 1.

The second Stillingfleet hinge (Fig.2) strikes a rather sombre Norman note, but is interesting in its use of decoration resembling a fleur-de-lis, a motif which persisted on hinges until the second half of the seventeenth century (Figs.7-9), being gradually replaced by simpler forms such as the spearhead, fish-tail or circular terminations.

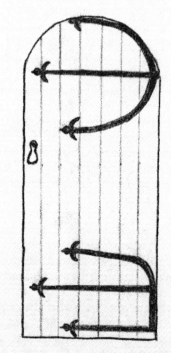

Fig 2.
St Helen's (West)
Church door,
Stillingfleet, Yorks.
1145

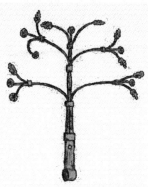

Fig 3. St Mary's Church Priest' Door, Morpeth, Northumberland. 1345

Fourteenth century hinges (mainly ecclesiastical) displayed flowing leaf and floral terminations (Figs.3,4), or adopted simple strap forms which relied on chiselled marks or hammered chamfered edges for ornament (Figs.5 and 6).

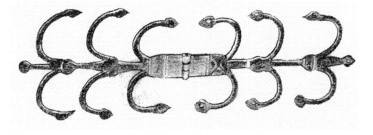

Fig 4. (Above) St. Mary's Church, Morpeth, Northumberland. C1350

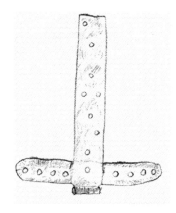

Fig 5. (Left) South door, Polstead church, Suffolk. 14C

Fig 6. (Below) South door, St. Mary's Church, Hadleigh, Suffolk. 14C

The spearhead termination (Fig.10) seems to have appeared in the sixteenth century (6) and it lasted for a hundred years in the north-east for substantial door hinges. Old, hand-forged specimens, are thinner at the spearhead, where the hot metal has been spread out on the anvil, whereas the body of the hinge usually consists of iron of uniform thickness; sometimes a down-turned tip is formed on the spearhead to assist in the initial placing of the hinge; genuinely old hinges will be fixed by wrought iron nails, and if the nail holes can be observed, they will be seen to have been punched rather than drilled into the hinge.

Cross-garnet hinges (Figs.9,11,12,13) were noted by Salzman (11) in a document of 1275. He quotes a reference in 1425 to potent garnets, a potent being a crutch. This refers to the T-shape of the hinge, which is the same as the cross-garnet, which is clearly illustrated by Moxon (9) in 1677. This type

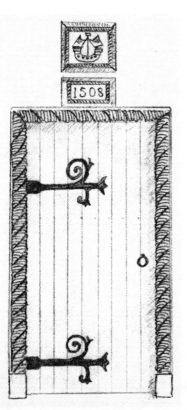

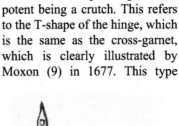

Fig 7. Saddell castle Keep door, Kintyre, West Scotland. 1508

Fig 8. Great Yarmouth. Pre. 17C

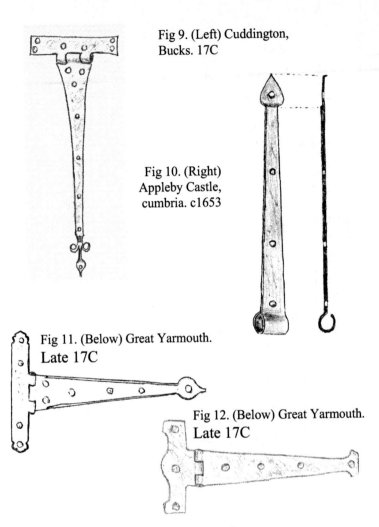

Fig 9. (Left) Cuddington, Bucks. 17C

Fig 10. (Right) Appleby Castle, cumbria. c1653

Fig 11. (Below) Great Yarmouth. Late 17C

Fig 12. (Below) Great Yarmouth. Late 17C

Fig 13. (Below) Great Yarmouth. Late 17C

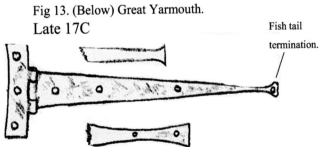

Fish tail termination.

occurs throughout the seventeenth century, with various tip terminations, and has been seen in north-east locations up to at least 1732. Identification of old cross-garnets is the same as for hook hinges - especially look for fixing with hand wrought nails.

The cross-garnet has been copied up to the present day, when it is called a strap hinge in building work. Towards the late eighteenth century, mechanical production techniques made hinges in thinner, smoother metal, with clean-cut fixing holes, readily differentiated from the older hand-wrought article. Victorian Gothic reproductions tend to over-elaboration with swelling profiles, bevelled edges and even polished finishes.

Salzman noted references in 1344 to a strap-less hinge for which the pinplate and the hanging plate were identical. It was called a gemels or gemews, and the description fits that of the H-hinges illustrated (Figs.14,15,17,18). The earliest illustration, of a fifteenth century type (Fig.14), shows punched decoration typical of that period (7), and it contrasts with the seventeenth century simplicity of the example from Harvington Hall (Fig.15). The H-shape was

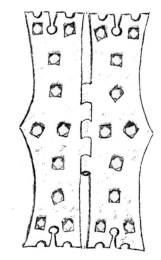

Fig 14. Boston, Lincs. 15C

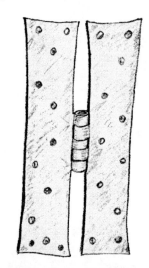

Fig 15. Harvington Hall, Worcs. Early 17C

sometimes elaborated into the highly decorative cockshead hinge (Fig.16), which was popular from the late-sixteenth century to the middle of the seventeenth century, being a typically late-Elizabethan and

Jacobean style. A northern example, dated 1653, occurs in Appleby, and appears to be near the end of its date range. Light-duty H-hinges, suitable for shutters or lightweight doors, were often refined with bevelled edges and shaped ends (Fig.17) between 1650 and 1720. The later tendency was to simple rectangular forms (Fig.18); cheaper and quicker to produce. These met the growing demands of the Great Rebuilding. With the advent of the Industrial Revolution in the late eighteenth century, cast iron butt hinges became the natural replacement for H-hinges.

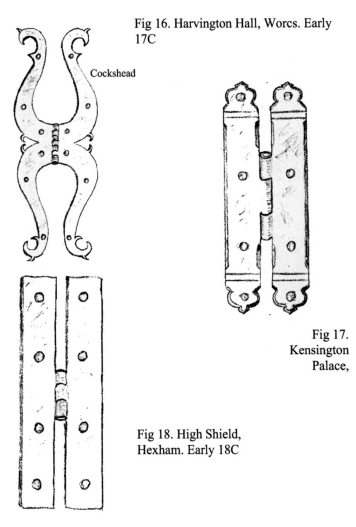

Fig 16. Harvington Hall, Worcs. Early 17C

Cockshead

Fig 17. Kensington Palace,

Fig 18. High Shield, Hexham. Early 18C

The butterfly hinge (Fig.19) was illustrated by Moxon in 1677, where he called it the duf-tail from its resemblance to a dovetail joint. It was a derivative of the H-hinge, used for cupboard doors, shutters, or similar light duties. The earliest mention which I have found is by Hodgetts(5) who noted a butterfly hinge on the entrance to a priest-hole built c.1590, and they have been noted in the north on shutters as late as 1758. They were most popular in the period from the late seventeenth century to the early eighteenth century.

H-L hinges are an adaptation of the H-hinge (Fig.20), where the tip of one arm has been extended at right angles to form an L-shape for the hanging plate. This adaptation was devised to reinforce the corners of the panelled doors, which progressively came into fashion during the seventeenth century, using quite light construction methods towards 1700. They appear to have gone out of fashion for important doors
about the middle of the eighteenth century. This may have been due to the use of thicker, more solid doors. Alternatively, the invention of the countersunk screw, and the use of butt hinges, may be the more likely cause (7). Fig.21 illustrates what is probably a Victorian Gothic reproduction, showing punched work characteristic of the fifteenth century applied to a seventeenth century type of hinge.

Various hybrid or combination hinges can be seen in different parts of the country. Not surprisingly, they occur at similar dates to their component parts. Fig.22 shows typical examples of a duf-tail combined with a strap hinge, and a hinge which is part H and part duf-tail.In the late eighteenth century hinges ceased to be treated as decorative features, and cast-iron butt hinges, similar to those of the present day, came into use. Screw-fixing replaced nailing. Fig.23 shows a typical rectangular type used in place of the butterfly hinge for shutters and small doors; this is useful for dating shutters in the late 1760's onwards.

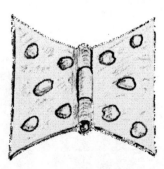

Fig 19. High
Shield, Hexham,
and Rievaulx
Abbey, Yorks.
Late 16C to 17C

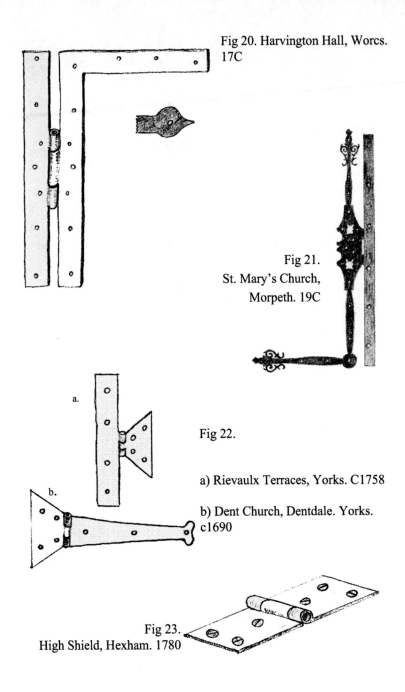

Fig 20. Harvington Hall, Worcs. 17C

Fig 21.
St. Mary's Church,
Morpeth. 19C

a.

Fig 22.

a) Rievaulx Terraces, Yorks. C1758

b.

b) Dent Church, Dentdale. Yorks. c1690

Fig 23.
High Shield, Hexham. 1780

Figs.24 to 27 show the combinations of chisel and punch marks typical of the decoration of small early hinges used for cupboards and chests. The simplification for the eighteenth century example is characteristic.

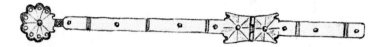

Fig 24. 15C

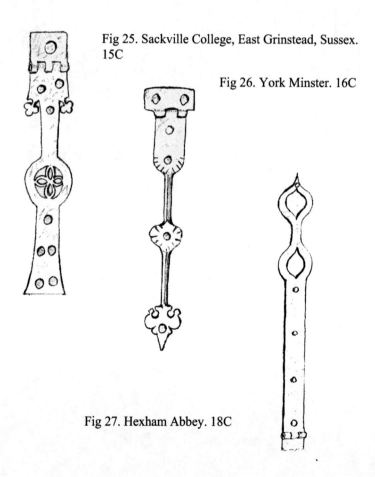

Fig 25. Sackville College, East Grinstead, Sussex. 15C

Fig 26. York Minster. 16C

Fig 27. Hexham Abbey. 18C

Miscellaneous Ironwork

The three door bolts illustrated (Figs.28 to 30) show the variability that can be found. Alcock and Hall (1) show many more from the seventeenth century.

It is difficult to detect any stylistic points to enable them to be used for dating purposes, and only a remote chance comparison with a similar bolt

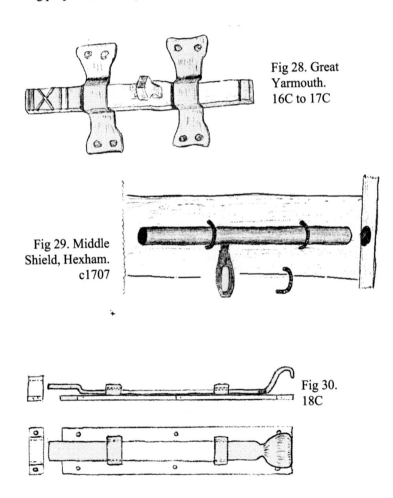

Fig 28. Great Yarmouth. 16C to 17C

Fig 29. Middle Shield, Hexham. c1707

Fig 30. 18C

from a house of known date is likely to be of help. The early eighteenth century bar-and-staple type noted in Hexham was apparently also in use in 1353 (11).

In a discussion of door locks Salzman (11) mentions a platelok of 1351. This type had the outer plate visible, and it was usually elaborately decorated. The book by Eras (3) shows many decorated European locks of this type from the fifteenth century onwards, but English examples are scarce. Spring-locks were in use by 1366, and stock-locks, which had the lock buried under a block of wood fastened to the door, were in use in 1357. These are occasionally noted, but probably need to be dismantled by a specialist to date them. Mortice locks were developed from 1770 and did not become widespread for a century (12). Rimlocks were common in the eighteenth century, and Miller (8) shows several locks of this type, particularly from the nineteenth century.

Lock displays may be seen in:-
The Science Museum
The Victoria and Albert Museum
The Bilston Museum in the West Midlands
J. H. Blakey and Sons, Church Street, Briarfield,
near Nelson, Lancs
The Lock Museum, 54 New Road, Willenhall.

Of the two latches illustrated (Fig.31), the earlier example shows the punched ornamentation typical of its period, while the later example shows the trend toward mechanical and artistic simplification. Alcock and Hall (1) should be studied for examples of dated latches and door handles.

Various metal-fixing devices for securing timbers are described in detail by Brunskill (2). He illustrates gibs and cotters, forelock bolts, stirrups and three-way straps are illustrated. Their utility for dating purposes will once more depend on comparison with local examples of known date in your locality. Gibs and cotters appeared just after 1700 (2). Hewett (4) mentions the occurrence of forelock bolts as early as 1225, and they continued in use to 1768 at least. Salzman noted a reference of 1532 to skrewis and vices which he suggested was the earliest reference to bolts and nuts. Screw-threaded nuts and bolts are reported by Hewett from 1661 (4). The single example illustrated (Fig.32) is from the early part of the eighteenth century, and it awaits accurate dating, being a key item in the dating of changes in an early seventeenth century house.

Bibliography

1. N.W. Alcock and L. Hall, Fixtures and Fittings in Dated Houses 1567-1763, 1994.
2. R.W. Brunskill, Timber Building in Britain, 1994.
3. V.J.M. Eras, Locks and Keys throughout the Ages, 1974.
4. G.A. Hewett, English Historic Carpentry, 1980.
5. M. Hodgetts, Secret Hiding Places, 1989.
6. H. Lander, House and Cottage Interiors, 1982.
7. J.S. Lindsay, An Anatomy of Wrought Iron 1000-1800 A.D.
8. J. and M. Miller, Period Details, 1993.
9. Moxon, Mechanick Exercises or the Doctrine of Handy-Works, 1677.
10. R. Neve, The City and Country Purchaser and Builders Dictionary, 1726.
11. L.F. Salzman, Building in England down to 1540, 1967.
12. M. Saunders, The Historic Home Owners Companion, 1987

Fig 31. Wooley, Allendale,
Northumberland. a)16C   b) Late 18C

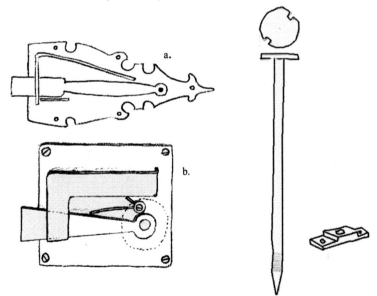

Fig 32. High Shield and George &
Dragon, Hexham.

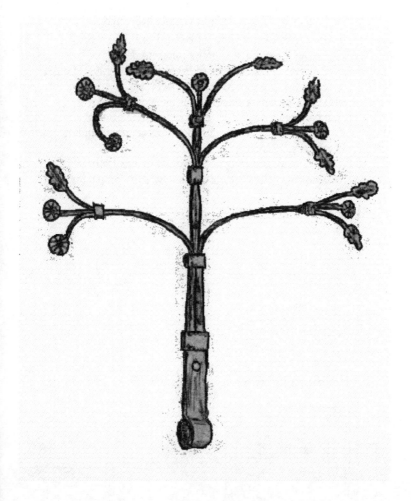

INTERIORS

Most house interiors are re-decorated at regular intervals for hygiene, or to meet the latest fashion; after twenty years one can tire of a particular wallpaper, or, worse still, it merges into the background and is never noticed, so failing to give the stimulus provided by colourful and pleasant surroundings. However, despite such constant change, medieval paintings have been known to appear from behind later layers of crumbling plaster, and the stripping of superimposed layers of wallpaper sometimes reveals fragments of a very early pattern which can be dated within twenty or thirty years. Old wallpapers also lurk unsuspected behind nailed-up shutters and in dark recesses. More permanent features such as moulded ceiling beams, panelled walls and decorative plaster all repay study. We attempt to bring these diverse items together and to provide a sufficient bibliography to show what is relevant for dating purposes when looking inside a room.

Starting with the floor, changes in level should be noted, as these can tell of a difference in building dates for the two levels. Ground floors were made of compacted earth from the earliest times and this usage persisted into the nineteenth century in humble dwellings. Commercial clay floor tile production started c.1280 in the South Midlands and Essex (3), and these were used together with paving stones in royal palaces and castles. Such substantial flooring had spread to manor house and farmhouse level by the fifteenth century, and was becoming general in the seventeenth century at domestic levels. Flagstones were used in stone areas, and brick laid on sand in stretcher bond or herringbone patterns was usual in brick-making areas. In eastern England, and particularly in Suffolk, clay tiles called pamments were used from the sixteenth century, laid directly in contact with the earth (4). Some coastal or riverside areas have very decorative floors made from pebbles set into patterns in sand (9). Where none of these materials were readily available, the compacted earth floors continued in use. By the beginning of the eighteenth century, boarded floors laid on joists, in direct contact with the ground, came into use for the parlour, other rooms retaining their simpler surface finishes. Problems with damp-induced rot gradually led to the development of the suspended timber floor later in the eighteenth century.

Upper floors were normally boarded from the time of their insertion into the hall house. However, in Derbyshire and the East Midlands, floors were often made of lime and ash, or gypsum, laid on reeds bridging the spaces between joists (Fig.1). These were typical of sixteenth and seventeenth century work (7), and have proved

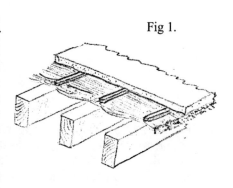

Fig 1.

surprisingly durable, lasting in many cases to the present day. Where boards were used, they were laid loose and could be removed if the occupier moved house; between the sixteenth and seventeenth centuries it became the normal practice for boards to be permanently nailed to the joists (7).

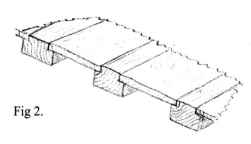

Fig 2.

Up to the sixteenth century, floorboards were normally laid parallel to the joists and rebated into them to give a level floor (Fig.2). The joists were normally of square cross-section up to c.1600, after which time cross-sections became gradually more rectangular, and slighter.

They were laid with the longer side vertical, and it was general practice for joists to be spaced wider apart with the floorboards crossing them at right angles (Fig.3).

Sawmills powered by water, wind or animals came into use in the sixteenth century (4), but most floorboards were cleft, to give fairly short

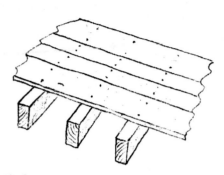

Fig 3.

lengths, or pit sawn to give greater lengths. Oak was the preferred material for the earliest floors; it cleaves readily, and boards were often over twelve inches wide and more than one inch thick. Elm was used, but less frequently; it does not cleave readily and had to be sawn. Firre deales were mentioned as early as 1641 in Hull (2), probably imported from one of the Hanseatic ports, and softwood gradually came into general use by the early eighteenth century. By the middle of that century, boards were typically eight to ten inches wide and over one inch thick (7). By the middle of the nineteenth century, widths from seven to nine inches with thicknesses of one inch were normal (2). An exception must be noted for better class floors which tended to use board widths of from three to five inches. The narrower planks shrank and warped less, leading to a closer fit between boards. Unfortunately, flooring details can only give the broadest of hints to dating. A typical Georgian house of 1787 exemplifies this in that it had oak boards for the parlour, white deal for the bedrooms, elm for the attic rooms, and stone flags or brick in the dairy (2).

Cold, plastered walls were insulated with painted wooden planks as early as the thirteenth century, when Henry III ordered his private rooms to be lined with wainscot (10). In the fifteenth century timber partition walls came into general use for substantial houses to separate private rooms from main living rooms (4). Timber lends itself to decoration, and the stylistic development of these walls from the fifteenth century to the middle of the eighteenth century gives a useful, if approximate, dating sequence. However, it is necessary to scrutinise panelling carefully to ensure, wherever possible, that it is original and not imported from an earlier building, as panelling, like window glazing, was treated initially as a removable fitting. Plain planks were used for the earliest wainscotting, but early fifteenth century partition walling was often made from shaped boards which fitted neatly into each other (Fig.4). At top and bottom the boards were tongued into horizontal rails; this system produced one very smooth face suitable for painted decoration, and one with a rippled surface. Examples from the fifteenth and sixteenth centuries were to be seen in Kent up to fifty years ago (10).

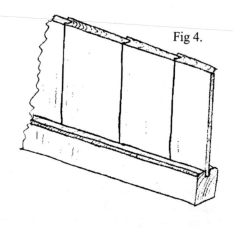

Fig 4.

Another early form of partitioning, dating from the fifteenth century, is that which is referred to as plank and muntin. It consisted of thick boards grooved into massive upright timbers called muntins (Fig.5). This was initially restricted to the larger houses, but had spread to smaller dwellings by the late sixteenth century, when more slender muntins were being used (Fig.6); plank and muntin partitions reached the true vernacular level in the middle of the seventeenth century (4), and continued in use for cottages into the nineteenth century (Fig.7). In Fig.6 the boards are shown tapering towards their edges, as it was easier to make a narrow groove in the muntin rather than making a rebate to take the full thickness of the plank. Lloyd (10) proposed that this raising of the centre of the plank, which in turn became elaborated into a rib, may have been the origin of the use of several decorative ribs on a plank, which in turn developed into linenfold panelling (Fig.8), which simulated the appearance of draped cloth on the panel. This style was popular between c.1500 and 1550 (7), although some authorities mention it as occurring from the late fifteenth century (9) to the early part of the seventeenth century (6).

Another development from the raised rib was the parchemin panel, named after the resemblance to a piece of folded parchment with curled corners (Fig.9). Simple forms of the late fifteenth century were succeeded by elaborate derivatives in the sixteenth century (10).

In the Elizabethan period, the tall panels made by vertical planks were split into a pair of smaller panels by a central horizontal rail (4), allowing shorter pieces of timber to be used for the separate panels. By the late sixteenth century, several horizontal rails were used producing small, nearly square, panels (Fig.10).

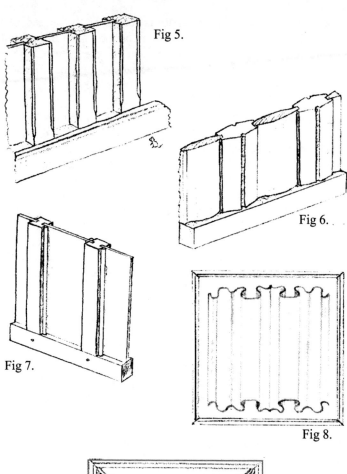

Fig 5.

Fig 6.

Fig 7.

Fig 8.

Fig 9.

Between the last quarter of the sixteenth century and the end of the Jacobean period, arcading (Fig.11) was a common form of decoration applied to these panels (9). The small, square type of panelling was becoming quite usual in farmhouses by the Jacobean period (2), and this style continued in use until the late seventeenth century (7).

Between the late fifteenth century and the early sixteenth it was normal practice to decorate the horizontal rails and vertical stiles of the panel framing with scribed lines or grooves (Fig.10). Later it became normal to remove the sharp edges of the frame by moulding them with a simple chamfer or more ornate form, and the problem then arose of how to treat the junction between the rail and stile. An early treatment is shown in Fig.12, where the mason's mitre, adopted from masonry work, has been used. This was changed to the true carpenter's mitre shown in Fig.13, as this was more simply made by moulding continuous lengths of timber, avoiding the hand-crafting required to fit a mason's mitre. Two authorities (10, 6) place the change from mason's to carpenter's mitre as c.1550, while others place it at 1600 (4) and 1650 (7), so this feature should be viewed with caution when dating. The differences of date may be attributable to the slow transfer of the technique from its use in grand houses down to the vernacular level. Towards the middle of the seventeenth century the problem was neatly and economically solved by applying mitred strips of moulding to the panels instead of moulding the framing members (Fig.14). This change is, unfortunately, difficult to detect by visual inspection unless glue between the strips and the panels has separated.

In the second half of the seventeenth century, imported pine and deal were increasingly used for the larger panels which became fashionable in important buildings. The proportions of the panels were strictly defined according to classical principles, the composition from skirting board up to the cornice at ceiling level corresponding to the structure of a column from the plinth upwards (Fig.15). Bulbous bolection mouldings surrounded the raised and fielded panels of important rooms, this fashion lasting until c.1730 (7). Throughout the eighteenth century, an alternative to the heavy bolection mouldings was for mouldings to become progressively less bold and more refined (6). By the late eighteenth century, panelling was being displaced in favour of plaster wall decoration; by c.1760 it was reduced to skirting board and dado, and by c.1770 only a skirting and chair rail remained (7). The mouldings used on skirting boards, panels, dadoes and door and window surrounds should always be inspected when trying to date a house, but as an inspection of

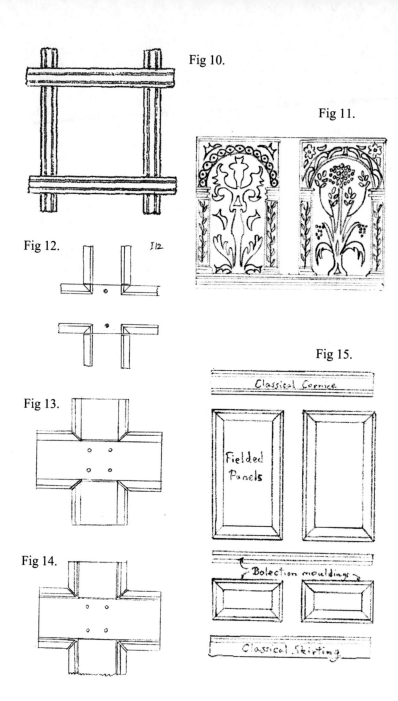

Fig 10.

Fig 11.

Fig 12.

Fig 13.

Fig 14.

Fig 15.

Classical Cornice

Fielded Panels

Bolection mouldings

Classical Skirting

103

examples in Lloyd (10) readily shows, there can be great variability in these features. Usually the details are most useful in working out the sequence of changes in particular parts of a house. In the author's house, six changes in skirting board patterns can be seen from alterations made over three hundred years; although accurate dates are only available for two changes in the twentieth century, four can be placed in sequence in the eighteenth century by a study of the mouldings and associated structural changes.

In the early seventeenth century, ornamental plasterwork appeared in smaller houses (2). The chimney breast or the space between the top of the panelling and the ceiling were typical areas to be decorated. Most examples are likely to date from the last thirty years of the seventeenth century, when external pargetting was very popular. After c.1725, large houses began to use plasterwork decoration, often of very elaborate, rococo forms, in place of panelling on walls (10). More elegant, restrained designs appeared after c.1770, under the influence of Adam, but by this time wallpaper was competing strongly as the most popular method of decorating walls.

This brings us to the consideration of the ephemeral types of wall decoration, from painted plaster or wood, tapestry and painted cloths, to the earliest wallpaper, found in Christ's College, Cambridge in 1509. The fascinating study of these developments can be followed in Ayres (2), Lloyd (10), Gray (7), and in other books in the bibliography, but as they are only rarely available to assist in our purpose of dating, they are not here discussed in detail.

If exposed ceiling beams are visible, they should be inspected to ascertain how they relate to chimneys and to any timber-framing. If the beams are later than the main framing, they may show that a floor has been inserted in an earlier hall house. A quick check for smoke-blackened beams in the roof could confirm this supposition. From the fourteenth to the early seventeenth century, beams were sometimes richly moulded along their lengths. A tentative guide to the dating of these mouldings is offered in Fig.16, but work by Jones and Smith (8) suggests that there is too much variation for this to be regarded as more than a very approximate method. Chamfers and mouldings were normally stopped, before they reached the wall at the ends of the beam, with an ornamental flourish, referred to as a chamfer stop (Fig.17). Many examples may be studied in the literature (8,1), but the variations seem too great for a systematic classification by date to be attempted.

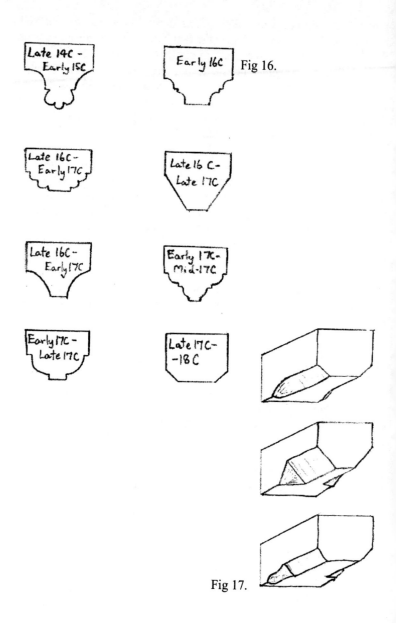

Late 14C – Early 15C

Early 16C   Fig 16.

Late 16C – Early 17C

Late 16 C – Late 17C

Late 16C – Early 17C

Early 17C – Mid-17C

Early 17C – Late 17C

Late 17C – –18 C

Fig 17.

Plaster was laid between ceiling beams during the sixteenth century to obscure the flooring above, and in the first half of the seventeenth century the main beams were also encased in plaster (2). Around 1600, it became the practice in vernacular houses to obscure the ceiling beams with a continuous plaster ceiling, and by the eighteenth century exposed beams were rare except in the smaller houses and cottages (6). The space between the ceiling and the floor above was often insulated with chaff, chopped straw or even cockle or walnut shells.

Ornamental plaster ceilings came into use in great houses during the sixteenth century, and the fashion spread to important smaller houses towards the end of the seventeenth century. The ceilings of vernacular houses remained plain. By the last quarter of the eighteenth century, plaster decoration tended to concentrate on a lavish cornice, with a rose in the centre of the ceiling, and this was the most common practice throughout the nineteenth century. Stylistic changes in plaster ceilings are useful for dating purposes, but they should be studied by reference to photographic illustrations, which can best display the intricate details. Lander (9), Lloyd (10) and Miller (11) have been found particularly useful.

Bibliography

1. N.W. Alcock and L. Hall, Fixtures and Fittings in Dated Houses 1567-1763, 1994.
2. J. Ayres, The Home in Britain, 1981.
3. J. Blair and N. Ramsey, English Medieval Industries, 1991
4. R.J. Brown, Timber-Framed Buildings of England, 1990.
5. O. Cook, The English House through Seven Centuries, 1984.
6. P. Cunnington, How Old is Your House? 1988.
7. E. Gray, The British House, 1994.
8. S.R. Jones and J.T. Smith, Vernacular Architecture, Vol.2, 1970-71.
9. H. Lander, House and Cottage Interiors, 1982.
10. N. Lloyd, A History of the English House, 1931.
11. J. and M. Miller, Period Details, 1990.
12. A.V. Sugden and J.L. Edmondson, A History of English Wallpaper, 1590 to 1914.
>13. C. Taylor, Wallpaper, 1991 (Shire).

MASONRY

The saying that the devil is in the detail is particularly apposite when attempts are made to date vernacular stone buildings. The details discussed apply specifically to the Hexham area, although some seem to be relevant over a much wider area, especially those for the end of the nineteenth century. The best that stone details can give is a time range within twenty or thirty years; some details may only suggest the earliest possible date for the feature, while others such as toolmarks may only bring the date to the right century. However, combined with more readily detectable features such as a doorway, such information may indicate whether the doorway is original or an addition to an earlier building, perhaps justifying further investigation.

The first thing to be noted is how the stone walls of the building are constructed. Rough field stones can be fitted together to form random rubble walls (Fig.1), or an attempt at greater regularity can be produced in rubble brought to courses (Fig.2). These are typical of seventeenth century vernacular work and low quality buildings at later dates. Very coarse-textured, light-coloured lime mortar was a characteristic of this stonework. In the eighteenth century, greater prosperity allowed the use of squared, coursed rubble (Fig.3) and rough ashlar (Fig.4). The ashlar blocks were of regular sizes, worked to a level surface, but toolmarks were still readily visible on the exposed faces. Fine ashlar work, with consistently-sized blocks of stone, very smoothly surfaced, and set with very fine jointing, was used in high quality buildings from early times, but the advent of improved stone-cutting methods allowed its use for humbler buildings in the nineteenth century. Snecked stonework (Fig.5) was frowned upon for the neat Georgian house, but between 1860 and 1880 it came into common use as a pleasant textural variant to ashlar which had come to be seen as somewhat bland and lacking in character.

Fig 1.

Fig 2.

Fig 3.

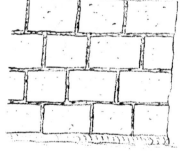

Fig 4.

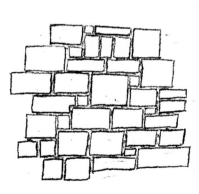

Fig 5.

In stonework with any aspiration to quality, some attempt was made to flatten the exposed surface, removing excess stone with cutting tools of various shapes, which left characteristic patterns of toolmarks. Toolmarks on Hexham stones will illustrate the principles. Seventeenth century quoin stones were usually brought to a level finish, but most show little, if any, toolmarking. The sandstone has a textured surface which suggests that centuries of frost action have spalled off the outermost layers of stone, removing with them any toolmarks. Some early eighteenth century quoins appear to have been levelled with a pick (Fig.6). By the middle of the century the pick was

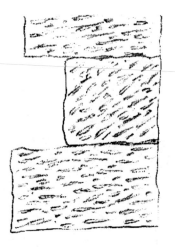

Fig 6.

replaced by a square-ended chisel. The marks show very limited attempts to orientate the blows of the tool along the length of the stone, resulting in a rough surface finish (Fig.7). Towards the end of the eighteenth century, quoins were flattened by a pattern of closely-spaced, parallel chisel marks (Fig.8), and this technique persisted through the nineteenth century, except where a smooth surface was achieved by further working of the stone with a drag (1). About 1825, it became common practice to make a neatly chiselled margin around the exposed surfaces of quoin stones and lintels. The central areas between these outer margins were filled with small, randomly spaced holes using a technique known as sparrow-pecking. This pattern is a clear indication of work of 1825 or later (Fig.9). Other tooling patterns such as combing have been noted on nineteenth century buildings, but no systematic dating can be ascribed to them. However, by 1880 the surface finish shown in Fig.7 had evolved to a very noticeable style in which the toolmarks were made along the length of the stone block in a regular manner (Fig.10). This style, possibly produced by machine, was in vogue for at least twenty years. About the same time (1880) rock-faced stonework came into use, and, as with snecking, the intention was to add interest to the wall texture (Fig.11). This style continued in use into the present century.

110

Fig 7.

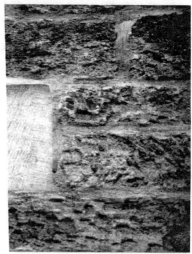

Fig 8.

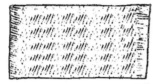

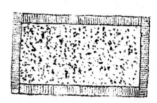

Fig 9.

Fig 10.

Fig 11.

A final aspect to note with stonework is any special shaping of individual pieces of stone. In this category comes the practice noted in this area from about 1700, of bevelling the edges of quoin stones, and setting them proud of the main face of the building, especially if it is brick built. Variations to the shapes of stone window lintels are noted in the chapter on Windows. Further variations on this theme, for buildings c.1880 and later, are shown in Fig.12.

It is repeated that this chapter is about stone buildings in a specific area. In other areas, practices will be different, but the principles are the same. Note every feature of the stonework, wherever dated buildings are found, and build up the pattern for your area. The limited data obtained may be crucial for a particular dating problem. Neglect nothing when dating!

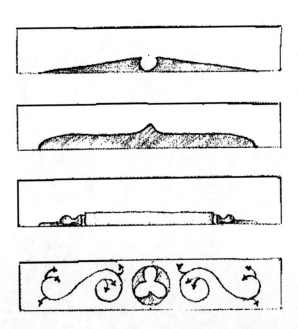

Fig 12.

ROOFS

Roofs rarely provide conclusive dating evidence, unless, perhaps, a dendrochronological trial can be carried out on their timbers, but any small clues combined with all other evidence from a house may prove crucial in an investigation. Fig.1 shows four of the most common roof shapes. As a general rule, a very steep pitch suggests the original use of thatch on a roof. Changes in the pitch of a roof, to provide extra headroom on upper floors, were generally possible when improvements in transport brought slate or tiles into an area. Disturbed stonework on the front facade or gable end of a house will show that such a change has taken place. The addition of an extra floor was also a common practice for older houses in the eighteenth

Fig 1.

Above - Saddled or Gabled.

Below - Hipped. Early 18C onwards

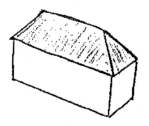

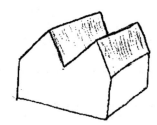

Above - Sawtooth or Double Span.
Late 17C to Late 18C

Below - Gambrel.

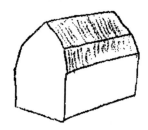

and nineteenth centuries, and the opportunity was taken to change the roof pitch and covering.

Early houses were only one room in width, with a gabled roof. One theory tells that this was due to the limit imposed by the length of timbers available for vernacular dwellings. Another theory suggests that the shutters, which preceded window glass, were closed on the windward side of the house, and the distance which light could penetrate from the open shutters on the lee side limited the width of the house. However, in Northumberland in houses of the eighteenth century, and later, windows were infrequently found on the rear facade to improve weather protection, and the house was orientated to face south-east to give the maximum benefit from sun and wind protection. The timber-size theory may be given some credence because the double-span house, with the sawtooth profile, was the most commonly adopted shape in the early stages of the Great Rebuilding, which started in the late sixteenth century in the south-east, spreading to the north of England by the early eighteenth century (8).

Hipped roofs occurred as early as the thirteenth century and were typical of the timber-framed Wealden houses of the fifteenth century; they gave a smooth outline which protected their thatch from wind damage. This style was again common from the middle of the seventeenth century to the end of the Queen Anne period, when it fell from popularity until the Regency. It finally had a long period of popularity between the two World Wars, characterised by ribbon development along the arterial roads.

Gambrel roofs were used in the sixteenth century, and became common on larger houses from the late seventeenth century (8). In the later part of the eighteenth century they were commonly adopted for small houses (10) to enhance storage space and sleeping accommodation, and the fashion for them revived in the second half of the nineteenth century (6). The distinction to be made between the gambrel roof and the somewhat similar Mansard roof (Fig.2) is clearly described by Johnson (9). The Mansard had dormor windows, whereas the Gambrel roof had windows in the gable end.

Specific roof features, such as projecting wooden eaves, and cornices supported by small blocks, called modillions (Fig.3), were prohibited by a London statute in 1707, to reduce fire risks, and by c.1710 parapets (Fig.4) were replacing them in the south (3). These were backed by wooden gutters lined with lead or pitch, to dispose of rainwater. Similar gutters

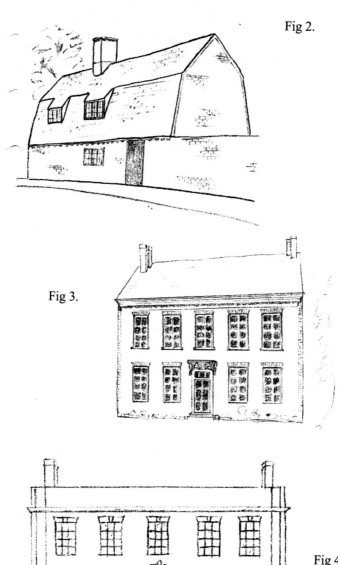

Fig 2.

Fig 3.

Fig 4.

were sometimes used on roofs that had no parapets, with a row of stone corbels acting as supports. These supports are occasionally found, disused, on a house where the roof has been raised. These may date from eighteenth century in the north, but elsewhere from c.1860. Rainwater gutters and downpipes were mandatory in London from c.1670, and lead versions became common countrywide from the middle of the eighteenth century. A bye-law in York made their use compulsory in 1763, and this emphasises the point that dates on rainwater equipment do not necessarily give the date of the building. Cast iron replaced lead for general use in the nineteenth century. Lead flashings for slate and tile roofs came into general use during the eighteenth or nineteenth centuries, depending on the area.

The pitch of a roof is determined by the materials which are used to cover it. If the pitch is steeper than seems appropriate for the slates or tiles covering it, the building was probably once covered with thatch, and is older than the present covering may suggest. The Table at the end of this chapter brings together information from several sources, showing the range of roof pitches for different roof coverings, and the probable earliest dates for the use of those materials.

Interiors of roofs are often the least altered part of a house, and no opportunity should be missed to investigate; even a wavering torch shining through an opened trapdoor can show whether there is oak or softwood, sawn or in its rough state, and interesting joints in a truss may prompt further investigation. A change of roof pitch can be inferred where alterations to a joint can be seen at the collar or apex of a truss. The change from oak to softwoods was a gradual process; Salzman (11) speaks of deal (deles de firre) being used in 1468, but the general change from oak to softwoods took place in the late seventeenth century or later, depending on local transport conditions. The specialist books on timber-framed buildings (1,2) show how a detailed investigation of roof structures and joints may date a structure, but many joints can only be fully revealed by dismantling the timbers. Roof designs became plainer in the eighteenth century, and simple A-trusses with a collar beam were typical in the north for stone-built houses. A half-lap dovetail (Fig.5) in better quality work c.1700, and raised crucks in the late seventeenth century (Fig.6), are examples of specific items of dating interest in the Hexham area.

Irregular saw marks, indicating pit-sawn timbers, and adze marks, can often be seen by shining a torch nearly parallel to the surface of a beam. Brunskill (2) gives dates for the introduction of power saws, the marks

Fig 5.
Typical Northern
Truss.

Half lap
dovetail.

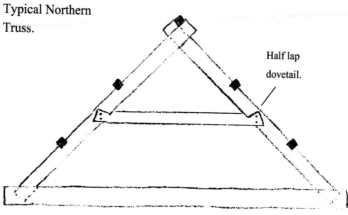

Fig 6.
Raised Cruck.

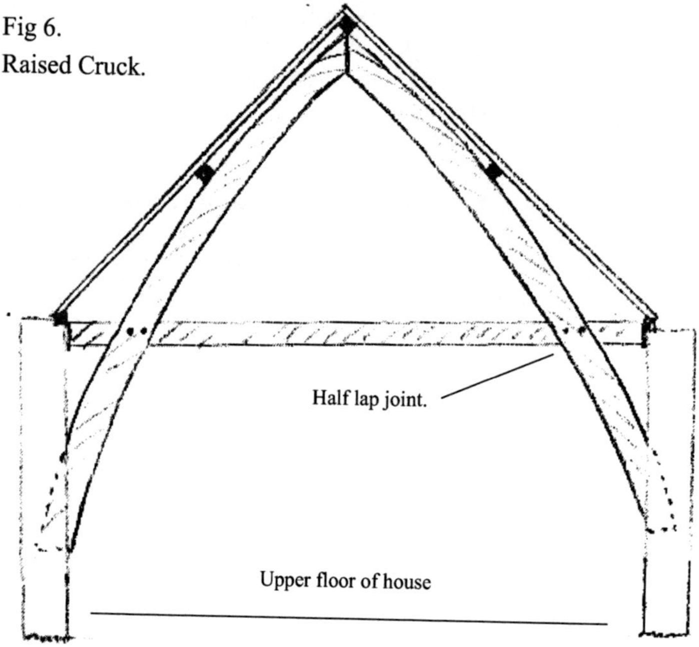

Half lap joint.

Upper floor of house

from which are normally much more regular than for the earlier hand sawn timbers. Wooden pegs (cylindrical or tapering) or metal fixings (2) can also be useful for comparisons in some areas. Again, in the Hexham area, a particular type of hand-wrought bolt with a keyed head (Fig.7) has only been noted for buildings c.1700 for a limited time range. Common rafters are sometimes worth notice as in some areas they were of square cross-section or wider than deep, until the late seventeenth century. After this, they became deeper and narrower (4); typical sizes were 21/2" x 2" at sixteen inch centres from 1800 to 1950.

Carpenters' marks (Fig.8) are worth seeking, wherever two timbers are joined. Roof trusses were dismantled, after being made in the carpenter's yard, and these marks were a guide to re-assembly at the house. The marks were used to the end of the seventeenth century and later in certain areas (4). Early marks were sweeping scratches made with a race knife. In the seventeenth century, gouges, chisels or knives were used, and by the eighteenth century small, deep chisel cuts were considered sufficient. Reference should be made to Brunskill (2) for full details and illustrations. Roof trusses were numbered in sequence, the truss at the socially important end of the house being numbered first. When trusses are found to be numbered out of sequence, it may mean that the roof has been altered at some time after its construction.

Roof dating is a tenuous process at best, but if knowledge of roofs in your own locality is gradually built up, by observing dated examples whenever possible, it becomes possible to develop an intuitive feel which can supplement observations elsewhere in a house. As a scientist, I recognise that this is unscientific, but, then, dating is often an art as much as science!

Fig 7.

Fig 9.

1	2	3	4	5	6	7	8	9	10
I	II	III	IIII	V	VI	VII	VIII	VIIII	X
ᐱ	Iᐱ	IIᐱ			∧	∧I	∧II	∧III	∧IIII
ᐱ	Iᐱ	IIᐱ			N				
etc									

11	12	13	14	15	16	17	18	19	20
XI	XII	XIII	XIIII	XV	XVI	XVII	XVIII	XVIIII	X̸
IX	IIX	IIIX	IIIIX	XV	IXV	IIXV	IIIXV	IIIIXV	X̸
			X̸I						

21	25	30
X̸I	X̸V	X̸X̸
	X̸VI	X̸X̸I

Slate
S Sandstone flags
L Limestone flags

Distribution of roofing
stones.

TABLES OF ROOFING MATERIALS.
PITCHES AND OCCURENCES

THATCH
Occurence -Most areas. Less where stone predominates.
Usual Pitch -50° -60°
Minimum Pitch -45°
Earliest Occurence -c500 B.C.? Forbidden 1212 in London because of fire risk. Forbidden again after the Great Fire of London in 1666.
Comments -Where thatch replaced by tiles, courses of stone or brick well above the later roof line on chimney stacks and adjacent walls, give evidence of earlier use of thatch. General View of Agriculture of Northumberland. 1805 -"Thatch, which used to be the universal covefing, has nearly fallen into disuse for cottage roofs."

OAK SHINGLES
Occurence -Mainly S.E. England
Usual Pitch -45° Steeper on church spires.
Minimum Pitch -45°
Earliest Occurence -"On many roofs in 13C." (10). Shown in Bayeux Tapestry (6). Used in Roman times (7).
Comments -Most common on church spires or modern, timber-framed dwellings. All apparently old ones must be replacements. Shortage of timber reduced their use in the Middle Ages.

LEAD SHEET
Occurence -Not normally for vernacular use.
Usual Pitch -Flat or with minimum angle for drainage.
Minimum Pitch -Flat
Earliest Occurence -Mentioned at Lindisfarne in 7C. Throughout Middle Ages. Increasingly after 1500 (11)

STONE SLATES
Occurence -Weald, West Country, Pennines, Lake District, Wales.
Usual Pitch -45°, Down to 30°, 30° or less, 30° to 35°, 35° to 40°
Minimum Pitch -Large (20°), Medium (25°), Small (30°), Small Thick (35°)
Size -Graduated; smallest in highest courses.

COTSWOLD SLATES
Occurence -Cotswolds and surroundings.
Usual Pitch -45° to 55°, even over 60° replacng thatch.
Minimum Pitch -45°
Earliest Occurence -Probably Middle Ages.
Size -Graduated; smallest in highest courses.

PLAIN TILES
Occurence -Brick clay areas. S. Derbyshire/E. Staffs.
Usual Pitch -50° to 60°/40° to 45°
Minimum Pitch -Normally 45°
Earliest Occurence -From 12C or earlier. By 14C in Somerset, York and Denbigh (13). Standard in London by 1500. Uncommon elsewhere before 1580. Dutch tiles available 1620.
Size -Regulated (1477) to 10½" x 6¼" x $^5/_8$"
Comments -Gradually replaced by slates after 1760 as transport improved. Nibs on tiles are known from 14C. Only widespread from 19C (10). In Kent the fixing hole becomes larger for the older tiles.

PANTILES
Occurence -East Coast/Bridgewater areas predominantly.
Usual Pitch -30° to 55°/35° to 40° normally.
Minimum Pitch -25° with 'torching.'
Earliest Occurence -From Holland c1630. Hull production from c1700. Bristol production from c1670. Earliest E. Anglian 'blacks' 1770
Size -Act of 1725 -13½" x 9½" x ½"
Comments -EnglishContinental (5).

'ROMAN TILES' (Singles & Doubles).
Occurence -Gloucester and Somerset.
Usual Pitch -Probably as for Pantiles.
Earliest Occurence -Bridgewater from 19C (11).
Comments -Roman tiles.Spanish tiles.

WELSH TILES
Occurence -Universal
Usual Pitch -Down to 30°. Usually steeper for resthetics.
Minimum Pitch -22° (1).
Earliest Occurence -Chester from 14C. Rapid growth from cI760.
Size -Normally uniform. Graduated in Wales near to the quarries.

Bibliography

R.J. Brown, Timber-Framed Buildings of England, 1990.
2.R.W. Brunskill, Timber Building in Britain, 1994.
3.O. Cook, The English House through Seven Centuries, 1984.
4.P. Cunnington, How Old is Your House? 1980.
5.N. Davey, A History of Building Materials, 1961.
6.E. Gray, The British House, 1994.
7.B. Graysmith, Tracing the History of your House, 1991.
8.D. Iredale and J. Barrett, Discovering Your Old House, 1991
9.B.H. Johnson, Vernacular Architecture Vol.22, 1991.
10.C. Powell, Discovering Cottage Architecture, 1984.
11.L.F. Salzrnan, Building in England down to 1540, 1967.
12.M. Saunders, The Historic House Owners Companion, 1987.
13.J. Blair and N. Ramsay, English Medieval Industries, 1991.

STAIRCASES

Early staircases (Fig.1) were mainly variations on the ladder, and very few examples are still to be seen.

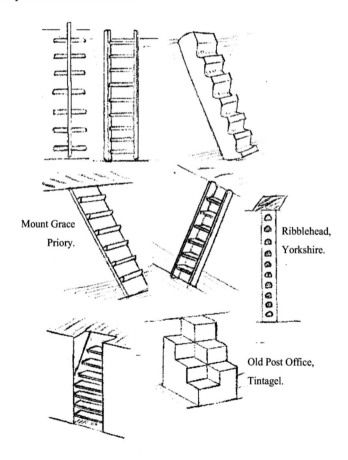

Mount Grace Priory.

Ribblehead, Yorkshire.

Old Post Office, Tintagel.

Circular newel stairs were one of the earliest types of what can be thought of as a real staircase (Fig.2); they were common from medieval times in castles and substantial houses, and transferred down the social scale over the years. In the late seventeenth century winding staircases in a rear projection were a feature of longhouses in North Yorkshire. They persisted in Scotland to the nineteenth century where they were commonly used in multi-storey tenements. When chimneys came into general use in the sixteenth century, they were frequently placed in the centre of the house. With the removal of smoke, it became possible to insert an extra floor to give rooms in a second storey, and access to this floor was gained by building a winding stair between the chimney and the front entrance lobby, or between it and the rear wall (Fig.3). This type was used in cottages up to the nineteenth century.

Fig 2.

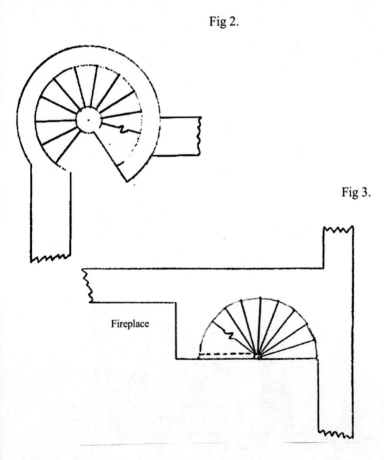

Fig 3.

Fireplace

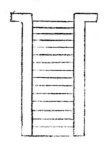

Fig 4.
From 16C

A straight flight of stairs built into the thickness of a wall was common in major buildings such as castles from medieval times (Fig.4); this form became common in small dwellings from the sixteenth century. The dog-leg staircase (Fig.5) came into use c.1575. It took more space than a newel stair, but allowed a more gradual ascent than this or a straight flight; a very marked characteristic of many late-seventeenth century dog-leg stairs is the very 'easy going' as this gradual ascent is called. This type became fairly common by 1630 in the south, and it was virtually standard for moderate vernacular dwellings by 1660, and it remained a very commonly used type for the next two centuries or more (2). Some areas were resistant to change and the dog-leg probably came into use after 1700 in the Lake District (2). Concurrently with the dog-leg a form of newel stair consisting of straight flights, built around a solid masonry core (Fig.6), came into use until the early part of the seventeenth century.

The open newel or open well staircase (Fig.7) came into use at the same time, and it soon superseded the solid-cored type as it offered greater scope for display. Its use was mainly in substantial houses which could afford space for its installation.

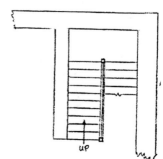

Fig 5. (Above). From late 16C

Fig 6. Late 16C to early 17C

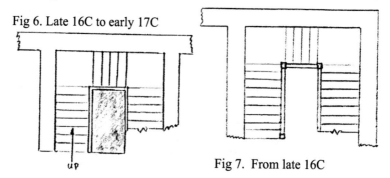

Fig 7. From late 16C

125

The parts of a dog-leg and an open-newel staircase are shown in Fig.8. The following illustrations show how each of these six components changed in the seventeenth and eighteenth centuries to give dateable sequences, which should (ideally) coincide to give a date for a staircase and, in turn, a date for an important stage in the development of the house.

Fig 8.

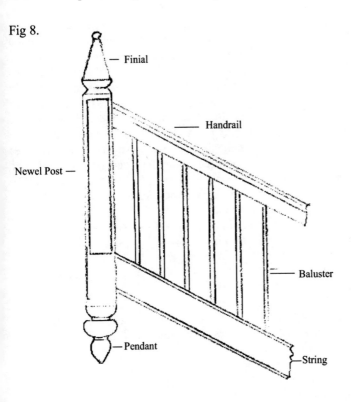

There was always considerable overlap in time in the adoption of the various styles, and so dates given can only give a very approximate guide. Fig.9a shows a profile of the heavy, square-section newel posts which were common from the late sixteenth century, surviving to c.1730 in vernacular dwellings. In 'polite' dwellings, newel surfaces were decorated with carved strapwork and other late Elizabethan and Jacobean motifs, in the first third of the seventeenth century (Fig.9b). These surface forms of carving were replaced by highly ornate carved work about the middle of the century; this vogue retained popularity for ten or twenty years. In the late seventeenth century, c.1670 until c.1700, newel posts were decorated with recessed panels (Fig.9c) outlined by various simple mouldings. This form had been seen as early as 1599 (1) but had been sparingly used before 1670. Square newels returned to favour between 1875 and 1910 (2). In the early eighteenth century slim, turned newel posts came into fashion (Fig.9d). The polite forms displayed flutes and carving to varying degrees. Newels were gradually replaced by groups of balusters supporting a curled handrail, from c.1725.

The staircase shown in Fig.10a, where the individual steps are obscured by a long piece of wood called a stringer, is a closed-string type. These came into use in the early sixteenth century and went out of favour about 1750; they were used again during the Queen Anne revival of the nineteenth century. The decoration of the stringer surface roughly paralleled that of the newel post. Early examples were plain, or decorated with a simple linear moulding (1), and for humble dwellings this continued as the standard form. Strapwork decoration was used in the Jacobean period in polite designs, and this was followed by Baroque carving (Fig.10b) in the middle of the seventeenth century. The late seventeenth century saw a variety of more elaborate linear mouldings (Fig.10c) than those used in the very early forms.

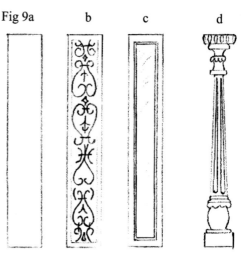

Fig 9a   b   c   d

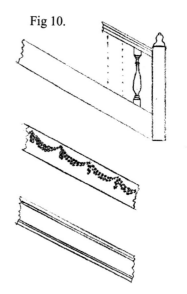

Fig 10.

From the beginning of the eighteenth century, the open-string staircase was becoming fashionable; each step was clearly visible in this form. The three types shown in Figs.11a to c were all current in the first thirty years of the eighteenth century. Figs.12a and b show other variants. 12b is a form much later on in the century when a desire for simplification led to the application of elegantly curved fretted forms to the ends of each tread. At this time, there was an increasing tendency to use the space under the staircase in vernacular dwellings, this being achieved by panelling under the stringer. In general, the decorative treatment of the tread-ends on an open-string staircase is not a sound feature to use for dating purposes.

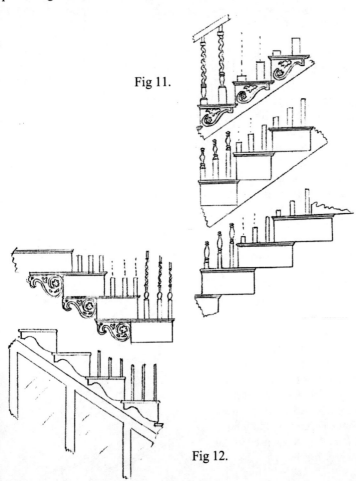

Fig 11.

Fig 12.

Fig 13.

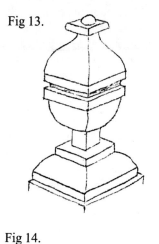

Finials were used to decorate the tops of newel posts from the late sixteenth century, if not earlier. Fig.13 illustrates an early finial, where the cross-section reflects the heavy square newel post underneath; this type probably dates from the late sixteenth century to the middle of the seventeenth. The spherical form, which can be seen to be latent in the shape of Fig.13, was commonly achieved from the middle of the seventeenth century when fully turned bun (Fig.14) or spherical (Fig.15) finials came into use. The spherical form was used from the late sixteenth century, but Fig.16 shows the earlier types which had small bases, were frequently not fully spherical, and normally had incised lines around the centre. Fig.17 is a type, intermediate between 13 and 15, corresponding to the first half of the seventeenth century.

Fig 14.

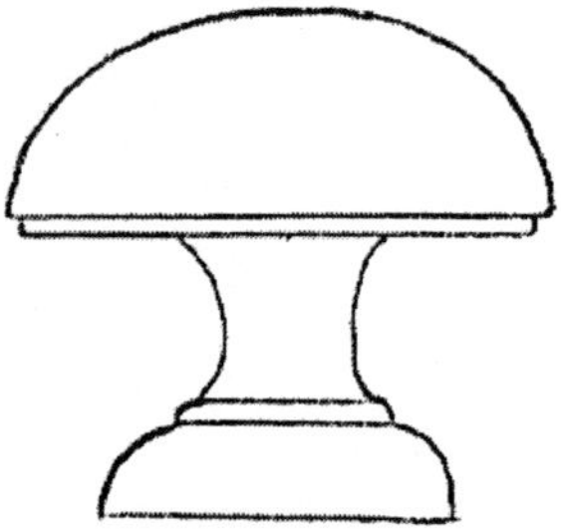

Fig 15.

Fig 16.

Fig 17.

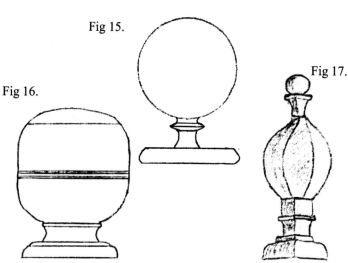

The elegant vase-shaped finial (Fig.18) was developed in the second half of the seventeenth century. Finials in polite houses showed much greater complexity. In the early seventeenth century, figures or heraldic beasts (Fig.19) adorned the tops of the newel posts. When the fully turned finials were developed they were often carved all over the turned surface with foliage or flowers; this fashion was used up to the end of the Commonwealth (1660). The vase form was similarly carved. Square flat tops, with an attempt at a classical form, came into use for newel posts towards the end of the seventeenth century (c.1670) (Fig.20), and finials went out of fashion until the revivalist styles of the Victorian era. Pendants are not described here in detail. Their forms tended to follow those of finials, frequently showing even more turned detail and complication. Alcock and Hall (10) show many examples.

Fig 18.

Fig 19.

Fig 20.

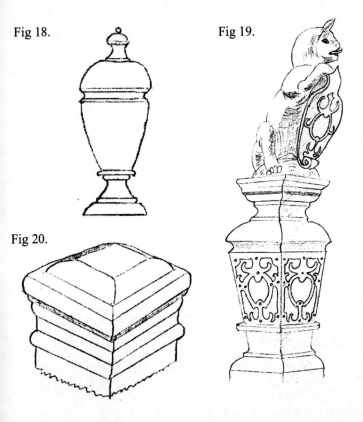

Early handrails tended to be deeper rather than wide (Fig.21), but later in the seventeenth century, when finials became unfashionable (c.1670), the broad style shown in Fig.22 was used more frequently as it merged smoothly into the flat caps of the newel posts. This style persisted in Cumbria to the late eighteenth century, but went out of vogue elsewhere. The thinner newels of the early eighteenth century required narrow, lighter handrails (Fig.23).

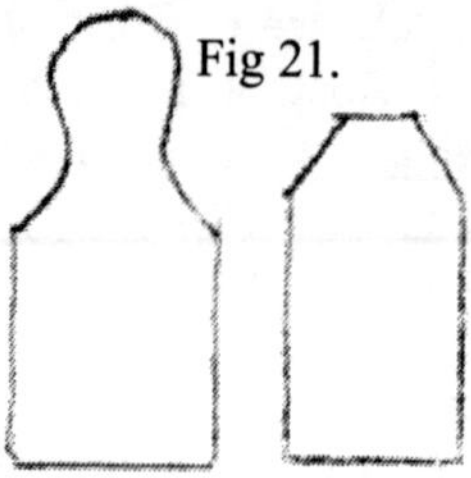

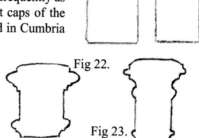

Fig 21.

Fig 22.

Fig 23.

The tendency through the eighteenth century continued to be towards simpler, lighter forms which permitted the use of the spiral (wreathed) terminations, until by 1770 plain section mahogany handrails were de rigeur for polite houses. Birch and pitch pine rails were used in vernacular work in place of mahogany. For detailed study of handrails Alcock and Hall (10) can again be recommended as an indispensable reference.

Balusters are the final staircase feature to be considered. Late sixteenth century bobbin balusters (Fig.24a) were stout, turned forms with diameters between 2 1/2" and 3 1/2" inches. Their sides tended to be parallel, with decoration being restricted to shallow, turned rings. The base of the baluster would have a square cross-section. An almost invariable feature of these early examples was a chamfer on each corner to merge the square section into the cylinder (1).

Another early type was the splat or fretted baluster (Fig.24c), cut out of flat planks of wood. Seen from

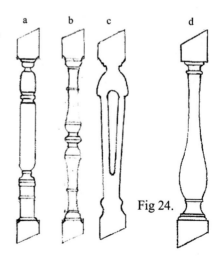

a   b   c   d

Fig 24.

the side, the profile of a splat resembled a turned shape with the centre fretted out. In polite houses the splat baluster was often thicker and elaborately carved, the centre fretted hole being omitted. Splats were in general use to the early eighteenth century. It was the simplest type of baluster to make, and it continued in use for humbler locations such as the servants staircase in the upper reaches of a house, and it was in vernacular use to the middle of the eighteenth century in North Yorkshire (2). It appeared again in revival work between 1875 and 1910 (2).

The vase baluster (Fig.24d) appeared c.1660, and was used with various turned embellishments into the early eighteenth century. Another form in this period is shown in Fig.24b. It shows the trend towards slim balusters which gradually occurred through the eighteenth century.

During the Commonwealth period, balusters were sometimes replaced in the more pretentious houses with heavily carved panelling, displaying acanthus leaves, fruit and heraldic motifs. This style continued in use to c.1670.

Barley-sugar twist balusters were first seen in 1652, but they came into common use c.1680 and remained in favour to the middle of the next century (Fig.25a). Early examples often used a small vase shape to terminate the base of the spiral. Georgian types sometimes used spiral fluting on a cylindrical baluster rather than making a full spiral. When stair

treads became wider, two or three balusters were mounted on each tread, and frequently a different form of spiral was used for each. One robust spiral per tread is the early form, c.1680, while three spiral balusters on one tread should be post-1700.

Fig 25.

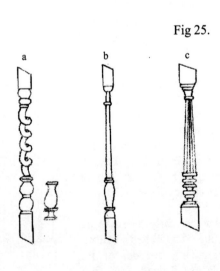

a   b   c

Very slim turned balusters (Fig.25b) were in use from the early eighteenth century, in keeping with the much slimmer handrails which were being used. Again it was common to see three of these balusters on each tread, and they were sometimes used in conjunction with barley-sugar twist types.

Fluted balusters (Fig.25c) were in fashion in the few years before and after 1730. It was a short-lived style.

Iron balustrades on stone staircases were very fashionable in the grander houses of the last quarter of the seventeenth century (1), but the style only became popular for smaller houses by the middle of the eighteenth century or later. Fig.26 shows the lyre shape which was common in the first quarter of the eighteenth century. By the Adam period, S-shapes (Fig.27) or types with anthemion or similar Adam motifs (Fig.28) came into use, and towards the late eighteenth century types reminiscent of the splat baluster were used (Figs.29,30). Turned balusters continued in use into the early nineteenth century. For vernacular houses, simple square balusters

Fig 26.(Above). St. Helen's House, Derby. Early 18C

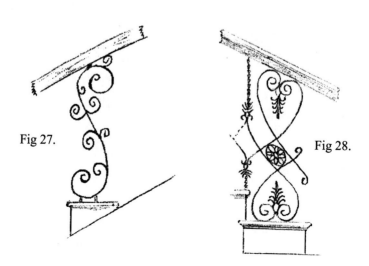

Fig 27.

Fig 28.

were the norm by 1770, remaining in use to the middle of the next century.

For further details concerning staircases, throughout this period, and onward into the nineteenth century, reference should be made to the glossary provided in the book by Gray (2), and to other books in the bibliography, especially Alcock and Hall (10) who show the wealth of invention which has gone into the elaboration of staircases in different parts of the land.

Bibliography

1.   W. Godfrey, The English Staircase, 1911.
2.   E. Gray, The British House, 1994.
3.   J. Ayres, The Shell Book of the Home in Britain, 1931.
4.   P. Cunnington, How Old is Your House? 1988.
5.   H. Lander, House and Cottage Interiors, 1982.
6.   N. Lloyd, A History of the English House, 1931.
7.   J. & M. Miller, Period Details, 1993.
8.   A. Quiney, Period Houses, 1989.
9.   R.C.O.H.M. York: Historic Buildings in the Central Area, 1981.
10.   N.W. Alcock and L. Hall, Fixtures and Fittings in Dated Houses 1567 - 1763.

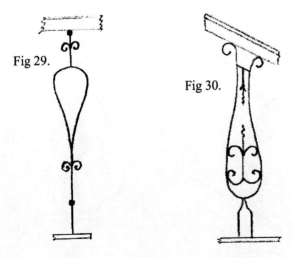

Fig 29.

Fig 30.

WALLS - EXTERNAL

Rendering.
This was used in several different forms for the following purposes:
Draught-proofing timber-framed buildings.
Covering porous or inferior brickwork and masonry.
Fireproofing timber-framed buildings - as in Bury St. Edmunds after the 1608 fire (4).
Decoration - see pargetting and ashlar in later sections.

Rendering conceals much dating information such as changes in wall height or fenestration, as well as earlier door openings, and it can be a source of great frustration.

Pargetting was a decorative form of wall rendering which used patterned plaster. Geometrical combed patterns were used in early work and in simple work throughout the period to the present day (Fig.1). Later

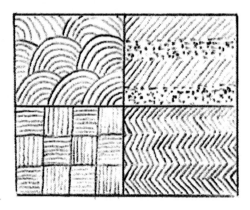

Fig 1.

developments used stamps to imprint patterns of flowers, animals, figures or heraldic motifs. Wooden moulds were also used to apply classical designs. According to Gray (7), the earliest dated pargetting is from 1530. It came into general use in the sixteenth century, with very decorative forms being developed between 1660 and 1670 with the exuberance which followed the accession of Charles II to the throne (Figs.2,3). The fashion declined rapidly after 1710.

Fig 2.
Cartouche

Fig 3. Floral Frieze. c1670

Periodic lime washing blurs the finer detail of patterns; if an example appears very crisp, suspect recent work or renewal of older work. The choice of motif can sometimes indicate modern vernacular revival work. In fact, a substantial proportion of what we see today is probably not original work, although it may faithfully copy the originals.

Harling is a Scottish rendering technique using a mixture of lime and unsorted river sand and gravel thrown on to the wall or applied with a small pointed trowel. The irregular material gives a liveliness to the surface. The only dating information noted for this technique is that some sixteenth century work incorporated fragments of glass into the aggregate giving a scintillating effect in sun or moonlight (13). Perhaps this is of limited dating use, but a nice feature to look out for. Naismith (10) indicates that harling was used on tower houses, which were common

136

from the fifteenth century, but much will date from early in the nineteenth century. Earlier work contained more lime and was softer in texture.

Stucco became very popular as a result of the 1774 Building Act, which virtually prohibited the use of exposed timber details on the outsides of buildings. It was a fine-grained render, based on lime and sand, but the term was generally applied to any of the patented cements such as Parkers cement and Coade stone which were developed to meet the new demand. They were all hand-applied by trowel. Stucco was usually scored with regular rectangular marks to give the appearance of ashlar stonework to inferior rubble or brick walls. Such ashlar markings occurred on internal walls from medieval times; an instance has been reported from Gonville and Caius chapel in Cambridge dated to the fourteenth century (15), and Celia Fiennes noted it on internal textural plasterwork in Norwich in 1698. This usage became common on external walls from the final third of the eighteenth century and continued to the middle of the nineteenth century (5). It can occasionally be seen in recent work.

Pebbledash uses sieved stone aggregate with a cement rendering. It is also referred to as roughcast or shingle dash. As the names imply, the mix was thrown onto the wall by hand or mechanically. The mechanical process and the uniform grading of the aggregate gave bland surfaces compared with harling. Roughcast buildings are known from the fifteenth century (5), but the process was in general use from 1850, and it was particularly common in England from 1890 to 1940 (7), especially on inferior brickwork. A novel variation noted on a 1930's bungalow in the north-east used a dash made of broken white marmalade jars. From 1950, spar dash render, which incorporates shining crystals of the mineral spar, became prevalent and is still used more frequently than pebbledash.

Cladding
Wall claddings served the same purposes as rendering, and were particularly used for weather protection. Some methods were used to circumvent the Brick Tax of 1784, while others were used to reduce the weight of a house, permitting lighter foundations to be used.

Tile-hanging consisted of tiles nailed directly to horizontal battens, or hung onto laths by projecting lugs or nibs to reduce the strain on the nails. As the style increased in popularity, decorative effects were achieved by varying the shapes and colours of the tiles (Fig.4). Simple tile-hanging for concealing or weatherproofing inferior walls started in Elizabethan times c.1590 (1). It became common in Kent after 1690, spreading over the south-east. As with roof tiles, older wall tiles tend to have larger fixing holes. Between 1784 and 1850 the Brick Tax boosted the popularity of this technique.

Slate-hanging was popular in the slate-producing areas from the mid-Georgian period, reaching a peak in the Regency (6).

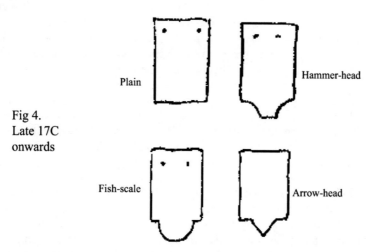

Fig 4.
Late 17C
onwards

Plain

Hammer-head

Fish-scale

Arrow-head

Weatherboarding or clapboarding used horizontal, overlapping boards to weatherproof walls. A weatherboarded gable was mentioned as early as 1321 (12), and a mention of wether-bord in 1515 is noted in the Historic House Owners Companion. Weatherboarding became common in East Anglia in the sixteenth century (8) and persisted intermittently to the present. Early work, on farm buildings, used oak or elm pegged to the structural framework with wood, as iron nails are corroded by oak. Elm was often left with an unsawn edge (referred to as waney-edged) as this protected it against rot.

Softwood imports began towards the end of the seventeenth century; softwood could be nailed to the framework. Protection was generally provided by pitch or whitewash. This cladding became very common when power-sawing began to produce planks in large quantities towards the end of the eighteenth century. Again, the Brick Tax could be avoided in this manner.

A neat groove, called a drip-stop, along the lower edge of a weatherboard, may indicate board dating from the eighteenth century, when this practice came into use (11).

Mathematical Tiles (Fig.5) occur mainly in south-east England, south of the Thames, but they are occasionally found in East Anglia and around Durham. They are a specially shaped form of interlocking tile which was fixed vertically to battens on a wall, giving the fashionable appearance of brick to a timber-framed house. A variety of other reasons for their use is given by Smith (19). They occur on buildings dating from the first quarter of the eighteenth century and were common from c.1760. The normal colour was red, but greys, whites and yellows were produced in the

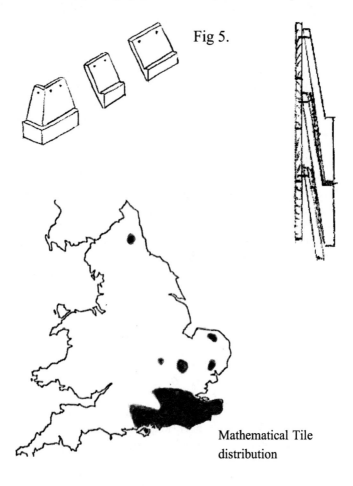

Fig 5.

Mathematical Tile
distribution

south-east in the second half of the Georgian period (c.1750), at the same time that brick colours were altered to simulate stone. Black tiles, used in Brighton to protect buildings from salt spray, date from the late eighteenth century. This dating data has been collected from Adela Wright's book (16), which gives a full treatment including details which help in differentiating mathematical tiles from ordinary brickwork.

Flints in complete or split forms have been used for building since Roman times. Saxon and Norman work used mixtures of flint, with rubble and fragments of brick embedded in mortar. It is most common in the south-east and south of England. In the thirteenth century roughly-coursed flints were used. Some were fractured (knapped) to make them more uniform in size. Complete walls of split flints were rare before 1290 (16). In the fourteenth century, flushwork was introduced. It was mainly used in ecclesiastical buildings. In this technique, flints were knapped to reveal the black shiny surface of the inside of the flint nodule. This was inlaid in a surround of carved, dressed stone to give highly decorative, patterned surfaces (Fig.6). The earliest example is probably at Butley Priory which was built in 1320. Humbler buildings showed neater coursing of the flints in this century (15) and squared knapped flints began to be used. Chequerwork patterns of flint and stone were introduced late in the century (5). This fashion continued in use at least until the seventeenth century (Fig.7).

Fifteenth century walling showed improving neatness and uniformity of the flints, even to the extent of giving uniform orientations to individual pebbles in a course (16). Chequerwork became more uniform, as in the excellent example at St. Osyth's Priory c.1475. Flushwork reached its peak in the middle of the fifteenth century, falling out of use in the mid-sixteenth century. Victorian church building renewed the technique in such splendid examples as the tower of Long Melford church.

The sixteenth century saw the continued use of flint. Late in the century, chequerwork became popular in Wiltshire, and this fashion lasted into the seventeenth century (6). Also late in the century was the introduction of bands of flint to decorate large chalkstone houses; this fashion was adopted for vernacular houses from c.1650 (9), (Fig.8). Flint continued in use to at least 1700 for small dwellings, as timber supplies became progressively more difficult to obtain (6). It was used in combination with brick dressings, as brick became more readily available towards the end of the seventeenth century (9), (Fig.9). The brick and flint were often

Fig 6.
Chalk and
Knapped
Flint.

Fig 7.
Flint
Flushwork.

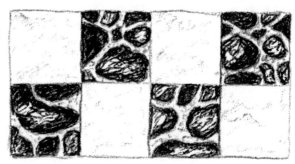

Fig 8.
Banded
Chalk and
Flint.

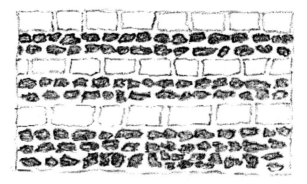

combined in an apparently random manner, giving most interesting visual effects in slanting sunlight, but, of course, this is not a dateable feature.

The only technical development in the eighteenth century appears to have been the introduction of knapped, squared flints for wall building (5). This was a very expensive technique (Fig.10). In the nineteenth century there was a revival of interest in vernacular building in the Regency and Victorian periods. Flint cobbles from the seashore became fashionable in the new seaside resorts. They were regularly-sized and coursed in the better quality buildings. Later in the century, colour and texture became important and flint was often used in conjunction with brick for a variety of decorative patterns (Fig.11).

Earth. Earth walls are always treated with some form of protective rendering and they are frequently lime or colour-washed. As a result it is not easy to identify this type of building. This probably accounts for the variety of dates given by different authorities for the occurrence of the different types of earth construction. The lists which follow quote the extreme date ranges which have been noted. All types of earth wall were normally built on a low stone wall to protect them from rising damp.

Cob is a carefully blended mix of clay and straw and it was used for building walls over a long period. In Devon, Dorset and Northampton, its use has been mentioned from the fourteenth century to 1850. The North Riding of Yorkshire saw its introduction in the late seventeenth century, and it arrived in Warwickshire in the early nineteenth century (14). The Yorkshire work was normally covered with a stone skin and so is only likely to be discovered during renovations. In the north west of England, cob is found between Carlisle and the Solway Firth, but, so far, no dating evidence has been found.

Clay lump is a mixture of clay, water and chopped straw which was moulded into large rectangular blocks (18" x 9" x 6") which were allowed to dry for several weeks before use. It is found in East Anglia, and is reported by several authorities to have originated in the seventeenth century. However, McCann (18) has clearly shown that the earliest use for house building in England was probably in 1792 in south Cambridgeshire.

Wichert was made from a band of hard, chalky earth found near Aylesbury. This was blended with water and straw in a process similar to that for cob. It was used up to c.1800 (8), mainly in Buckinghamshire.

Fig 9.
Brick and
Cobble
Chequers.

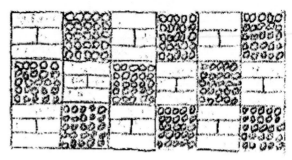

Fig 10.
Square
Knapped
Flint. Stone
Quoins.

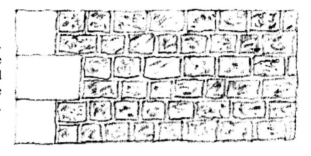

Fig 11.
Knapped
Flint with
Brick
Dressing.

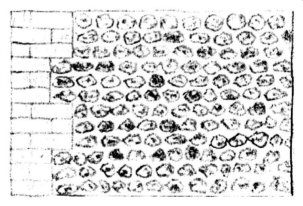

143

Timber framing (Fig.12)

Timber-framed buildings were divided into cruck and balloon-framed types. This section deals with the dating of the different patterns of framing to be seen on the external walls of these buildings.

Large-panel framing displayed large, open rectangular panels, about six feet in length. This was the most common form before c.1450, and it has been reported from the early thirteenth century (7). By 1500 it was only used in poorer houses or in the less important facades of larger houses. It was rarely used after 1550 (9). Various patterns of braces were used to stabilise these large panels, the earliest, in the late fourteenth century being the arch-braced frame, common in the Midlands and the west of England. By c.1525, tension-braced frames, which had been adopted earlier in the east and south-east, were being generally adopted. The St. Andrews cross type of bracing was in use from c.1330 until the end of the fifteenth century (7). Reference should be made to R.J. Brown (2) for a fuller treatment of bracing.

Fig 12. Timber Frame Recognition.

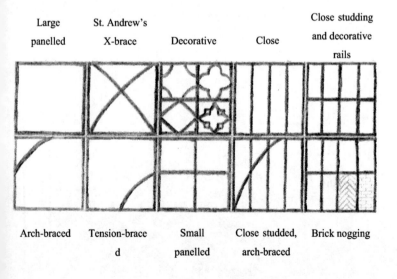

Large panelled	St. Andrew's X-brace	Decorative	Close	Close studding and decorative rails
Arch-braced	Tension-braced	Small panelled	Close studded, arch-braced	Brick nogging

Small framing or square framing appears as a grid of squares two to three feet across with two squares to the height of each storey of the house. This style appeared c.1450 in better class houses of the west and north-west areas, and it persisted to the late seventeenth century. It came into use for small houses in Cheshire, Kent and East Sussex in the middle of the sixteenth century and persisted to c.1700. From c.1570 to the early seventeenth century, the squares were decoratively infilled with elaborate motifs, especially in Cheshire and Lancashire. East Anglia was the only area that resisted this style (7).

Close-studding displayed close-set vertical timbers extending to the full height of each storey. This style probably originated in East Anglia in the early thirteenth century. It reached most towns in the early fifteenth century, and persisted well into the seventeenth century in East Anglia, where the conspicuous display of expensive timber served to enhance the status of the owner.

A modified style appeared in the west and the Highland zone c.1450, in which a middle rail was inserted halfway up the height of each storey. This enabled shorter studs to be used. This style was common in the sixteenth century and persisted into the seventeenth.

Jettying was the name given to the projection of an upper storey over the one below. The term is reputedly from the French jete meaning something thrown. Tiptofts Farm in Essex, dating from the late thirteenth century, is one of the earliest examples still extant (2); jettying was most popular from 1350 to 1620 in towns, at which time fire hazards led to their final fall from favour (8). Jetties occurred only sporadically in the country, and they had gone completely out of fashion by 1600.

Halls with cross wings at each end were erected from the late fourteenth century until the early sixteenth century, the Wealden houses of Kent being examples of this style. The cross wings were normally jettied. Single storey halls were usually made into two stories in the sixteenth century, by the insertion of a chimney and an intermediate floor. The continuous jetty house, jettied along the whole of the front of the house, then became common, and this style lasted into the seventeenth century (3).

Before 1450, the exposed ends of the joists in a jetty were protected by fascia boards (8), but then it became fashionable to expose the full structural details of the building, decorating them by elaborate carving.

The bressummer beam which spanned the ends of the beams in a jetty, while supporting the wall above, was carved with vine foliage, and corner posts and dragon beams were similarly decorated with figures. This fashion lasted into the sixteenth century.

Brick-nogging was the term used for the infilling of the panels of timber-framed buildings with brick instead of wattle and daub. A late fifteenth century wall-painting shows what is probably the earliest evidence of this technique (9). The bricks were arranged to give an interesting pattern, herring-bone being commonly adopted. Important houses showed brick-nogging in the late fifteenth century, and it spread into the south and east in the next century. It only became common for small houses c.1650 (9).

Low quality timber frames became more common in the seventeenth century as timber supplies became more difficult to obtain. They were usually concealed by plaster or some form of cladding. This low quality of construction continued into the nineteenth century in some areas.

This section concentrates on matters relevant to the dating of the exteriors of timber-framed buildings. For fuller illustrations reference should be made to the many authors in the bibliography, whose work is gratefully acknowledged. Brunskill and Harris are particularly useful for descriptions of internal timber work such as roof structures and flooring, but dating of these features is best carried out by the specialist technique of dendrochronology rather than by a study of stylistic detail.

Bibliography

1. Sir W. Addison, Farmhouses in the English Landscape.
2. R.J. Brown, English Farmhouses, 1982.
3. R.W. Brunskill, Timber Building in Britain, 1994.
4. A. Clifton Taylor, Six English Towns, 1985.
5. A. Clifton Taylor, The Pattern of English Building, 1965.
6. A Clifton Taylor and A.S. Ireson, English Stone Building, 1983.
7. E. Gray, The British House, 1994.
8. D. Iredale and J. Barret, Discovering Your Old House, 1991.
9. E. Mercer, English Vernacular Houses, 1975.
10. R.J. Naismith, Buildings of the Scottish Countryside, 1989.
11. J. Prizeman, Your House: The Outside View, 1975.

12. L.F. Salzman, Building in England down to 1540, 1967.
13. M. Saunders, The Historic House Owners Companion, 1987.
14. J.T. Smith and E.M. Yates, On the Dating of English Houses from External Evidence, 1968.
15. J.A. Wight, Brick Building in England, 1972.
16. A. Wright, Craft Techniques for Traditional Buildings, 1991.
17. Personal communication. R.M. Higgins Associates.
18. J. McCann, Vernacular Architecture, Vol.18, 1987.
19. T.P. Smith, Vernacular Architecture, Vol.10, 1979.
     R. Harris, Discovering Timber-framed Buildings.

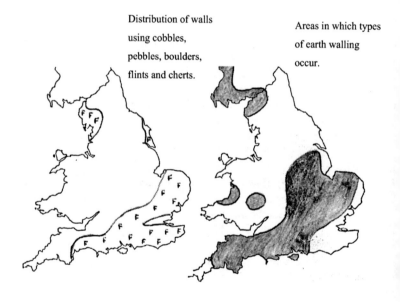

Distribution of walls using cobbles, pebbles, boulders, flints and cherts.

Areas in which types of earth walling occur.

Other maps showing the distributions of walling and roofing materials can be found in the Illustrated Handbook of Vernacular Architecture by R.W. Brunskill, 1971.

WINDOWS

When trying to read the date of a house, the windows appear to be an easy tool on which to base an educated guess, but we are up against the problem that house owners, for generations, seem to have wished to make a mark on their home. The result may be that a timber-framed house is encased in fashionable brick or a stone house is weatherproofed by rendering, and the opportunity is taken to alter the fenestration, with improved, maybe larger, windows. The Georgian desire for a symmetrical facade often eliminated mullioned seventeenth century windows in favour of the new-fangled sash window, the only tell-tale sign being asymmetrical chimneys which could not be altered so easily. Signs to look for are additions to the jambs at the side of a window, which allowed tall sash windows to replace shorter mullioned windows, without changing the width of the aperture; this feature on the upper windows of a house can show that the roof has been raised, or the angle has been altered with a change from thatch to Welsh slates. Sometimes lintels show a triangular mark in the centre. This shows that a mullion has been removed. This would have allowed the insertion of a Yorkshire sliding sash window to give better lighting and ventilation. Early sash windows, with thick glazing bars, were sometimes replaced at a later date with new sashes with very thin glazing bars to give more light, or merely to replace rotted timber. In such a case, an elegant surround to the central window frame, above the central entrance, would be a clue that the sash windows were originally installed in the early part of the eighteenth century when a different, more elaborate treatment was given to the central windows; the date of the later replacements may possibly be deduced from the pattern of window panes used. Use the following diagrams and their descriptive notes with circumspection, and enjoy the fun of reading a house. It must always be more often art than a science.

Notes to accompany Illustrations

1,2,3. (12C.) The semicircular arch supported by columns characterised Norman windows up to the last quarter of the twelfth century. Paired windows could have flat or semi-circular heads as shown, but they were always enclosed by the semi-circular arch. The so-called 'Jews House' and 'Norman House' at Lincoln show excellent examples.

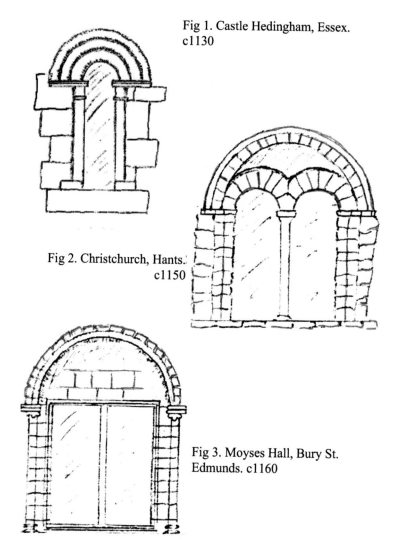

Fig 1. Castle Hedingham, Essex. c1130

Fig 2. Christchurch, Hants. c1150

Fig 3. Moyses Hall, Bury St. Edmunds. c1160

Fig 4. Stokesay Castle, Shropshire. 1291-1305

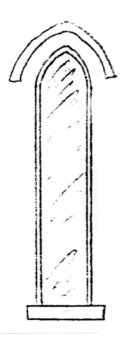

4,5. (Late 12C and 13C.) The pointed arch was first used in the Middle East in the seventh century A.D., from whence it was probably introduced to England by returning crusaders towards the end of the twelfth century (1). The Early English lancet window (Fig.4) was very tall and narrow, perhaps indicating an initial distrust of the structural security of the new form, but yet providing sufficient light by its length. Paired windows (Fig.5) gave greater illumination, but the structural leap to a single pointed window was not attempted. Extant examples of

Fig 5. Oakham Castle, Rutland. c1180

these window types are restricted to castles and halls and are only included to show the progressive development of window characteristics.

6,7. (13C.) In the early part of the thirteenth century, windows were decorated by plate tracery which involved ornamentation such as a quatrefoil being carved in the blank space between the two window heads and the containing arch. Later, this space was pierced, rather than being carved, thus admitting more light (9). The heads of the windows were initially decorated with rounded tracery, and in later examples this became pointed to produce cusped heads. The lower windows in Fig.6 would have been covered by shutters, while the upper sections may have been glazed.

150

Fig 6. The Great Hall, Winchester Castle, c1232-40

Fig 7. Little Wenham Hall, Suffolk.
C1260-80

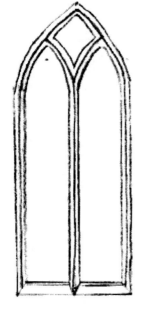

Fig 8. The Great Hall, Eltham Palace, Kent. 1479

8. (Late 13C to 15C.) A later development was a simplified form called Y-tracery.

9,10. (14C & 15C). Two variants of the ogee curve (S shape) were used in early fourteenth century tracery (Fig.9), but the most general feature was the use of the cinquefoil (five-lobed) window. (A useful mnemonic for this style is - Trefoil or Three lobes, Thirteenth century - cinquefoil or Five lobes, Fourteenth and Fifteenth centuries). The spandrels (triangular areas around the window openings) were emphasised by being sunken. The mullions (vertical bars) and transoms (horizontal bars) were thinned out to admit more light by splaying their sides. Characteristic examples occur in older manor houses.

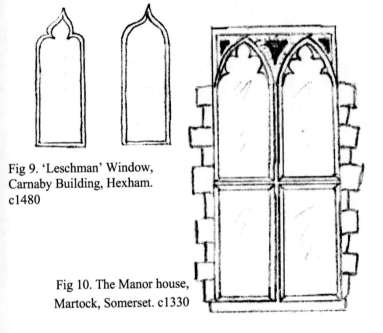

Fig 9. 'Leschman' Window,
Carnaby Building, Hexham.
c1480

Fig 10. The Manor house,
Martock, Somerset. c1330

11. (Early 14C to c.1380.) Decorated tracery of the type shown occurred during the fourteenth century, but its use for domestic work was limited. Church architecture shows many more examples.

12. (Late 14C to early 15C.) Drip moulds came into use over the top and sides of the window to throw rain off, and the mullions were extended vertically to strengthen the window. The extension to three lights is not a dating feature, as windows with up to five lights had occurred earlier.

152

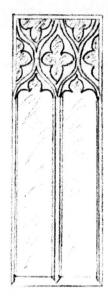

Fig 11. Northborough Manor, Cambs. c1340

Fig 12. The Manor house, Martock, Somerset.
Late 14C

13-16. (15C to mid 16C.)

Pointed windows were not always curvilinear, and triangular heads (Fig.13) occurred throughout the mediaeval period (9). However, the fifteenth century saw attempts to simplify window shapes to accommodate the increasingly popular stained glass.

Fig 13. A school at
Ewelme, Oxon. c1440

Fig.14 illustrates a late fifteenth century window, which gives a simpler shape for the main lights, but exhibits a style of tracery at the top which was in vogue for a very short period at the end of the century. Fig.15 shows the smooth flattened arch typical of the final third of the fifteenth century to c.1550. This basic unit was combined with similar units horizontally and vertically to make large windows typical of Tudor buildings (Fig.16). These windows were displayed in projecting bays which occur from c.1393 (12).

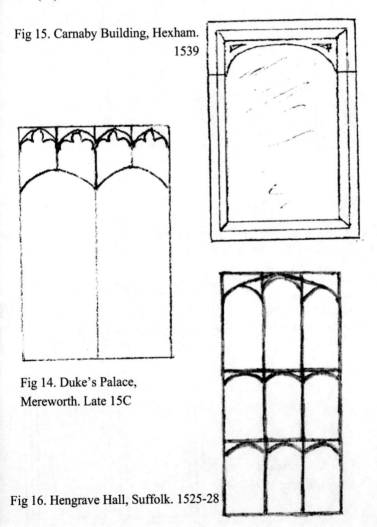

Fig 15. Carnaby Building, Hexham. 1539

Fig 14. Duke's Palace, Mereworth. Late 15C

Fig 16. Hengrave Hall, Suffolk. 1525-28

154

17. (Late 16C into early 17C.) The Tudor period saw the end of the Gothic style, and the simplification of window shapes to rectangular forms.

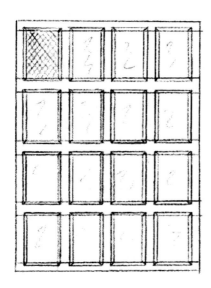

Fig 17. Late 16C to early 17C

Fig.17 shows a typical large Elizabethan mullioned and transomed window suitable for a manor house, where the window could be topped with a classical moulding or a dripstone. Hood moulds or dripstones were normal features for this type of window in the sixteenth and seventeenth centuries, serving for decoration and rain deflection. By the middle of the seventeenth century, the separate hood moulds over individual windows were normally merged into a continuous moulding linking all adjoining windows. This ascending and descending moulding gradually became a continuous horizontal string course. The cross-section of a mullion may give dating information. R.J. Brown (2) illustrates several different stone mullion cross-sections with date ranges for their occurrence. He suggests that mullions with glazing rebates date from the early seventeenth century. However, it must be pointed out that another authority differs by a hundred years for one style and it may be that there are wide regional differences. Opening casements of wrought iron or shutters were the normal method of obtaining ventilation; opening windows were mentioned at the chapel of Sherbourne Castle as early as 1250 (12). Occasionally decorative lead grilles were set into a section of the fixed glazing to give some ventilation. Casements were in general use until the introduction of sash windows, and they continued in use in humbler dwellings with low ceilings.

18. (16C to 19C.) The introduction of brick chimneys into medium-sized houses in the early part of the sixteenth century enabled an upper floor to be introduced into hall houses. Long, low windows replaced the tall

transomed windows, and the type in Fig.18 became common. Lights were normally grouped in pairs or larger numbers. For the larger groups, intermediate mullions were thickened to support the extended lintel. This type continued in use to c.1700 in the north east, and into the nineteenth century in Pennine weavers' cottages and in the Limestone belt.

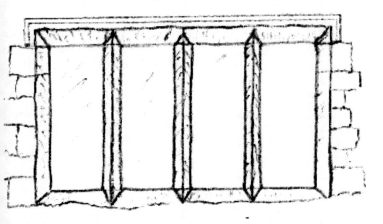

Fig 18. Local examples include Holy Island House, Hexham. 1657 (4 light windows), Ovingham Old Rectory, Late 17C (4 light windows), and Main Street, Corbridge, Jacobean, (3 light windows).

19. (16C & 17C.) Fig.19 illustrates the use of a transom for taller windows which were popular in the sixteenth century for farmhouses when it became usual to build higher rooms. It was customary for the two dimensions shown to be equal, the upper light being made shorter by an amount equal to the thickness of the transom.

Fig 19.

20. (17C to c.1800.) In the early seventeenth century, the cross window was introduced, with the transom placed higher. This style came into Northumberland c.1670 for perhaps twenty years, and it persisted in Lancashire and Cumberland almost to the end of the eighteenth century (6). The raised transom was probably introduced to give less obstructed views.

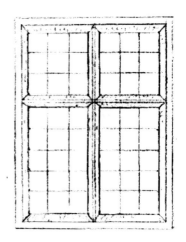

Fig 20.
The Deanery, Winchester,
Hampshire. Early 17C

21. (c.1700.) By the late seventeenth century, windows in houses below gentry rank were changing to squared surrounds (Fig.21), (13). The old drip mould has been developed to a more classical moulding over the windows; this feature is seen in several early eighteenth century houses in the Hexham area.

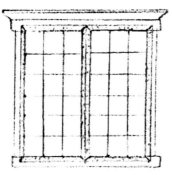

Fig 21.
Middle Shield, Hexham.
c1707-1720

22. (Early 18C to late 19C.) Various treatments of the square window are illustrated. Mullions were frequently removed to allow the use of the horizontally-sliding Yorkshire sash which rapidly became popular after its introduction, reputed to have been at Moss Farm near Doncaster in 1705 (2). The triangular mark left by the cutting of the mullion will indicate the earlier type of window. Hinged opening casements gave increased ventilation. They were initially glazed with small quarrels, but were usually fitted with glazing bars to conform to sash windows elsewhere in the house if these were present. Dating these window types is difficult, and depends on details such as thickness of glazing bars or the introduction of cast iron casements in the early nineteenth century (5). Wrought iron casements were available from at least 1600 (6).

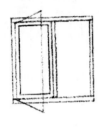

Fig 22.

Square, two-light window. One side-hung casement opens.

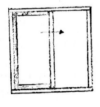

Yorkshire sliding sash. The left-hand sash slides horizontally behind the right-hand sash. Introduced at Moss Farm, near Doncaster in 1705. Very popular where ceilings are low.

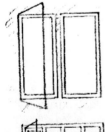

The mullion is retained, giving support in stone-built cottages, to the lintel. One casement pivots open.

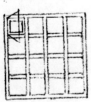

One small pane opening, and all others fixed.

158

23. (Mid 17C into 18C.) The West Riding window is a fairly localised modification of the standard mullion window; it may be considered as a hybrid between types 18 and 20. Fig.23 shows a window in Littondale dated 1650, into which larger panes of glass with wooden glazing bars were inserted at a later date, no doubt replacing a small-pane latticed window. Similar types occurred in Scotland up to c.1790 (6).

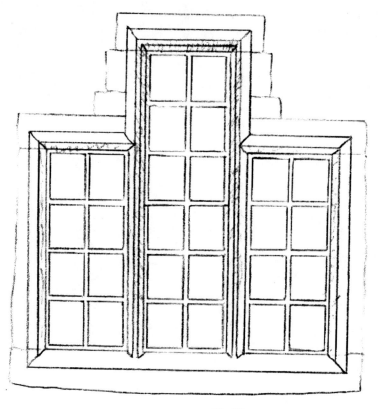

Fig 23.
Arncliffe, Littondale,
Yorkshire. 1650

24. (c.1670 onwards.) There was much experimentation with window design in the seventeenth century, and Fig.24 shows the Flemish type as seen in Sparrowe's House in Ipswich (c.1670). It was introduced c.1625 and faded from favour c.1710 (6). It was again used in the eclectic Victorian period between 1875 and 1905, and never fails to give distinction to the buildings in which it is used.

Fig 24.
Sparrowe's House,
Ipswitch. C1670.

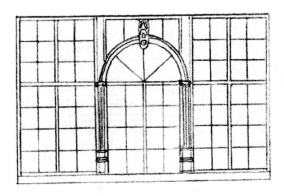

This type of
casement window
was fashionable in
East Anglia at the
end of the 17C.
Mentioned by
Pevsner at
Statham Hall,
Suffolk. Also to be seen locally in Yorkshire. (Settle, Boroughbridge).

Fig 25 (Below). Late 17C to early 18C

25. (Late 17C to early 18C.) Circular and oval windows with rubbed brick surrounds were in vogue in the Queen Anne period. However, they are mentioned by Pevsner as late seventeenth century in Norfolk, and Nathaniel Lloyd (9) illustrates examples dated as late as 1734. Gray (6) places them between 1670 and 1720.

26. (Late 17C to early 18C.) Dormer windows seem to have originated in the sixteenth century at the time that upper floors were being inserted in hall houses. From c.1680 to c.1720 a fashion developed to crown alternate dormers in a row with triangular or segmental pediments. This style occurred c.1650 at Coleshill House, Berkshire, but took some years before it came into common use.

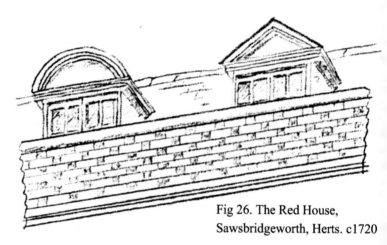

Fig 26. The Red House,
Sawsbridgeworth, Herts. c1720

27. (Early 18C.) Coupled or bi-partite windows appeared in the Queen Anne period, probably as a result of the 1696 Window Tax, which allowed windows in which the two components were separated by less than twelve inches to count as a single window (6). They occurred in limestone areas to the middle of the eighteenth century, and the style frequently occurs in the Yorkshire Dales and Cumbria. These windows became common in the late nineteenth century especially in the Newcastle area.

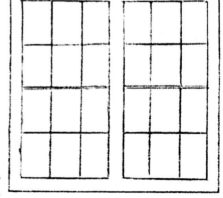

Fig 27. Queen Anne. Early 18C

161

28a-28c. (c.1690.) Shutters which would slide in the vertical plane are mentioned by William Horman in his Vulgaria of 1519. Vertically sliding windows were installed in royal apartments from 1662, these being supported in an open position by pins inserted into the window frame. The fully-fledged sash window, with sashes counterbalanced by lead weights, cords and pulleys, appeared c.1670 (8) and rapidly gained universal approval. The proportions of the windows in Figs.19 and 20 made it a simple proposition to replace them with sliding sashes. Figs.28a to 28c show the early experimentation in the development of the sash window as applied to Hampton Court (c.1690). Lower level, less important rooms were provided with relatively short sashes, with many small panes of glass, while windows on the upper, piano nobile, floor were tall and slender and were fitted with fewer larger panes. Servants living on the uppermost floor had to be content with small, squat windows fitted with a multitude of cheaper, smaller panes. The sash window rapidly evolved to consist of two rows of panes in each sash, either three or four panes wide. By c.1720, six-pane sashes were standard. This configuration lasted until the Regency period, in the early nineteenth century, when the desire for more light and the continuing effect of the Window Tax led to the re-introduction of eight-pane sashes. Sashes with six panes for the top and nine panes for the bottom may also date from this period. Oak was used for early sashes but it was soon superseded by softwoods.

29. (Early 18C to c.1750.) The early eighteenth century sash had an exposed wooden surround, which contained the counter-weight mechanism, flush with the face of the house. Glazing bars were nearly two inches wide, and the top sash was often a fixture; this can be seen when there is no timber bead to guide the sash downward. Fixed top sashes were seen until c.1750, and even later in very simple dwellings; they were used in Scotland at much later dates, possibly due to reduced ventilation requirements in the more boisterous climate.

30. (c.1680 to 1730.) Part of the early experimentation with the sash window was the use of the segmental head (Fig.30). By 1730, this style had been simplified to rectangular sashes with segmental brick arches to the windows, this being a cheaper form to produce (4). Windows with semicircular heads were used between c.1700 and 1720, and they occurred sporadically for over a hundred years, before again becoming very common in the late nineteenth century (10).

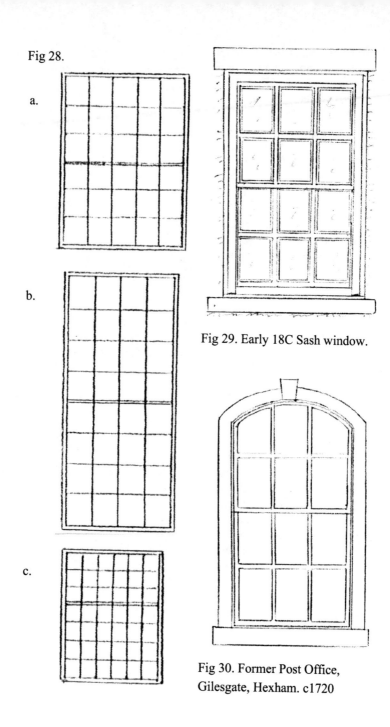

Fig 28.

a.

b.

c.

Fig 29. Early 18C Sash window.

Fig 30. Former Post Office,
Gilesgate, Hexham. c1720

31. (1709 onwards.) The illustration shows a sash window with its frame set back from the front surface of the house, as stipulated in the London Building Regulation of 1709. This requirement was designed to stop the spread of fire across the face of the building, and had the incidental benefit that the shadows which it produced helped to enhance the aesthetic effect of the windows. This feature, if seen, only sets an earliest date for a window of this type, as it took upwards of fifty years for this practice to spread to some parts of the country. By 1709, glazing bars were becoming more slender, (perhaps 1.25 inches), and both sashes were normally counterbalanced in the larger houses. Early pulleys for the sash cords were made of wood; they were generally replaced by metal pulleys by the last quarter of the eighteenth century.

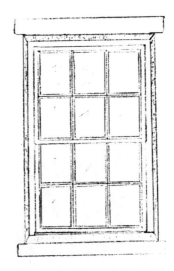

Fig 31. Mid 18C to c1840. Examples - High Shield, Hexham and Wooley Farm, Allendale.

32. (1774 onwards.) A further fire precaution, in the London Building Regulations of 1774, required that, in addition to the four-inch recess, the wooden window surround containing the counter-balance mechanism should be concealed behind the brick or stone of the window surround. As with style 31, this feature only gives a date later than the Act. By this time, glazing bars were as narrow as five-eighths of an inch; comprehensive details of how glazing bars changed in shape and size and material (wood, lead and cast iron) are given in a book

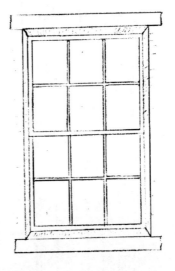

Fig 32. Late 18C through 19C

164

about fanlights (7). Lintels, whether of stone or brick, frequently had splayed ends in this period. Fasteners, to connect the meeting rails in the centre of the window were introduced c.1774. The Brooking Collection in Dartford Polytechnic contains many exhibits of old windows and their fittings dating from c.1660 to 1960, providing an invaluable source for detailed study of particular window features, especially in the eighteenth and nineteenth centuries.

33. (c.1730 to c.1790.) Pevsner noted a Venetian window (Fig.33) in Norfolk, dated 1622, as a total innovation for England. However this type seems to have come into fashion in the early eighteenth century; examples dated c.1730 are illustrated by Lloyd (9) and Clifton-Taylor (3), and the type was common up to c.1790 (6). The sashes in the centre could be opened in the normal manner. Ware (15) writing in 1756, laid down the rule that the side lights should not be narrower than the centre light. This rule was frequently flouted, but it may indicate an early date for a window which conforms to it.

Fig 33. Early 18C to c.
End of 19C. 'Venetian'
window. Example at
Burn Brae House,
Hexham. 1847?

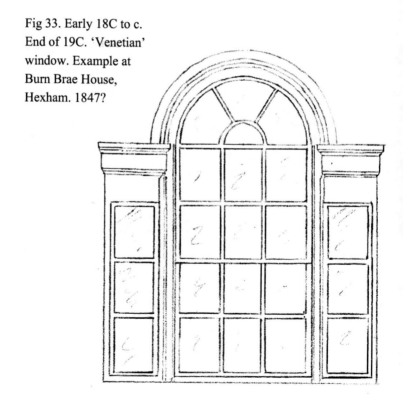

34. (c.1760 to mid 19C.) The 'thermal' or 'Diocletian' window is a type which was discovered in the thermal baths erected by the emperor Diocletian in Rome in 306 A.D. This type was adopted by the Adam brothers c.1763 and was in vogue until the end of the Regency period.

Fig 34. Mid 18C to c. Mid 19C. 'Diocletian' window. Example from Burn Brae House, Hexham, dated 1847.

35. (c.1760 to mid 19C.) The tri-partite, or Wyatt window, after the architect who popularised them, came into common use c.1765, possibly to counter the increased Window Tax. Their use was further enhanced in the Regency, and they continued to be popular well into the second half of the century. They were sometimes economically constructed by reusing earlier sash windows for the centre position, building these into the extended window. In this circumstance, the thickness of the glazing bars can be a misleading dating feature.

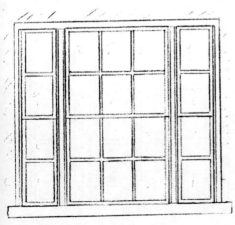

Fig 35. 1760 to Early 19C. Tripartite windows. (Wyatt Windows). Examples at Burn Brae House, Hexham, c1780, and Sele Gate House, Hexham.

36. (c.1750 to 1840.) Gothic windows, with intersecting tracery, and pointed arches came into fashion with the erection of Strawberry Hill near Twickenham c.1755. They had a long popularity until c.1840 (6). The style recurred sporadically at later dates.

37. (c.1780 to c.1825.) The sixteen-pane sash window reappeared about 1780, and was popular at least until the Window Tax was reduced in 1825.

38. (c.1820-1830.) A characteristic of the ten years from 1820 was the use of an arched recess with a sash window set back four inches from the inner brick surface. The sash boxes were fully concealed.

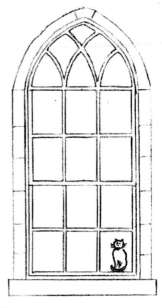

Fig 36. Late 18C to late 19C. Rochester Farm,

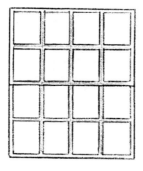

Fig 37. Middlemarch House, Hexham. 1792

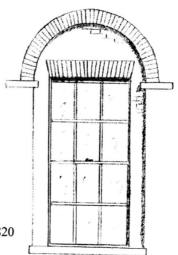

Fig 38. c1820

167

39. (c.1810 to c.1860.) The availability of larger sheets of glass probably accounted for the introduction of windows with larger central panes, and narrow margins, c.1810, as a change from the rigid uniformity of Georgian six-pane glazing. This type is variously referred to as bordered or margined, and persisted to c.1860.

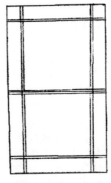

Fig 39. 'Bordered' sash. Early 19C

40. (c.1850 to c.1910.) The window of Fig.39 was simplified in the second half of the century by the removal of the horizontal glazing bars. This style was sometimes referred to as Oxford glazing.

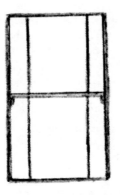

Fig 40. 'Oxford' glazing. C1850 - 1910. Ristorante Fortini, Hexham.

41. (c.1800-1870.) The lying-pane style of glazing was used in some spa and south-east towns during the Regency, and it was used in parts of Scotland from c.1825 (11).

Fig 41. 'Lying-pane' glazing.

168

42-44. (c.1835-1880.) Lucas Chance introduced the improved cylinder method of making glass from the continent in 1832 (7) and Figs.42 and 43 show how the larger panes of glass, which became available, altered the appearance of sash windows. The weight of large glass panes tended to damage the mortise joints on the lower corners of the top sash, and so downward extension pieces called horns were introduced for reinforcement. About 1880 glazing bars were replaced in the upper sash, and this style remained in favour until 1920 (6). The intention was to moderate the fading of furnishings by reducing the incoming sunlight.(Fig 44).

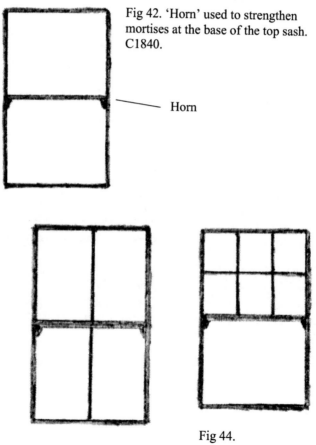

Fig 42. 'Horn' used to strengthen mortises at the base of the top sash. C1840.

—— Horn

Fig 44.

Fig 43.

45a-45n. These pictures of window lintels illustrate developments which mainly apply to the south of Northumberland over two centuries. Only certain styles are relevant elsewhere, but the series is intended to demonstrate the potential of such studies for dating purposes.

45a. Wood lintels were used into the early part of the eighteenth century for dwellings, and to later dates for farm buildings.

Fig 45a.

45b. Window surrounds made from single blocks of stone occurred from the late seventeenth century to the early eighteenth, particularly in the west of the area. They were much commoner and to a later date in Cumbria. The style was used in important buildings throughout the eighteenth century, with the stone being moulded to form elaborate architraves.

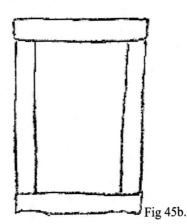

Fig 45b.

45c. Rectangular stone lintels were in vernacular use from the late seventeenth century. They were roughly smoothed, and tend to show few remaining tool marks, possibly due to weathering. Later in the eighteenth century the marking referred to as sparrow-pecking is sometimes seen.

Fig 45c.

45d. Rubbed brick lintels with serpentine shapes recessed in their lower edges are an early eighteenth century feature, which is very little noted in the north, as stone is the norm.

Fig 45d.

45e. Stone lintels with triple keystones appear to be a very early eighteenth century style in the area.

Fig 45e.

45f. Segmental brick arches over segment-headed windows were usual in the south from c.1710 to c.1730. After that date, straight lintels were normally used, although the segmental form persisted in the brick areas of the Midlands to c.1750.

Fig 45f.

45g. Splayed stone lintels came into use c.1760.

Fig 45g.

171

45h. Shows an interesting example of the change actually occurring in some structural alterations carried out in 1768.

Fig 45h.

45j. Lintels with Coade stone ornaments placed at the centre occurred from 1769. These are uncommon in Northumberland and are not illustrated here.

45k. Herring-bone tooling can be seen from Cumbria to North Yorkshire,

Fig 45k.

where it is especially common in the Whitby area. Dated examples have been noted from 1770 to 1992 and so this is not a feature of use for dating purposes.

45l. Stone lintels which show very regular saw marks may date from the late eighteenth century.

Fig 45l.

45m. Lintels with smooth or very neatly chisel-marked margins, and pecked faces first made an appearance in the area c.1825.

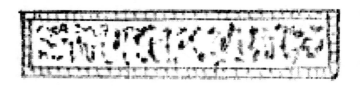

45n. A chamfer on the lower edge of a lintel, with neat stops at each end, is a characteristic from c.1880. A wide variety of more elaborate decorations of this sort originated about that date.

45o. A point not illustrated, but which may usefully be included, is that in the early part of the nineteenth century there was a short-lived fashion for attaching decorative iron grilles to the sills of upper floor windows (14).

Windows which protrude from the front of a house are not illustrated, but they include oriel windows, which project from above ground level. These occurred as early as 1442 in Rye House (16), and became common in the late fifteenth century. They are of little use in isolation as a dating feature. Bay windows project from ground level; they were known from 1393 (12), or more generally for grand houses from c.1450. In smaller houses, they became common from c.1750 and quite standard for speculative building from 1860 to 1940. Muthesius (10) and Gray(6) give full discussions of this form. Canted bays, which are flat-fronted, with the sides inclined at an angle to the wall, became common after the 1774 Building Act, which forbade the projection of a bay beyond a defined building line, to avoid obstruction to passers-by. Bow windows are curved rather than rectangular bays; they were used from 1760 (6), and were particularly popular at the end of the eighteenth century.

Toplights are fully discussed in a book entitled Fanlights (7), which gives many excellent illustrations. Fig.47 is adapted from their work to show the shapes and materials for some of the glazing bars used in the eighteenth and early nineteenth centuries. Other materials such as zinc and wrought iron were used, but the painting of glazing bars generally means that shape is the main feature that can be seen. Toplight glazing bars faced their moulded sides to the inside of the house in early examples, following the example of glazing bars on other windows. This was changed at an early date so that the more elaborate mouldings faced outward, as this was where they would have their maximum effect. This was in line with the principal doors which had their elegantly moulded sides facing the outside, where visitors could see them on arrival. The back of the door, which was rarely noted, was normally very plain. The date of this change was probably c.1720.

Toplights to doors were known from 1638 or earlier (6) and they became increasingly common from the beginning of the eighteenth century, when higher rooms demanded more light. Observation of many dated buildings, suggests that the rectangular type of toplight (Fig.46) was most common in the early eighteenth century, although occasional semi-circular examples may have occurred, especially when round-headed doors came in to use to match the round-headed windows of that time. The rectangular form persisted throughout the eighteenth century, and was particularly used in the Greek revival period of the early nineteenth century.

Fig 46. c1725.

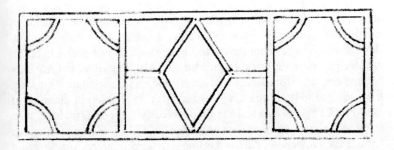

174

Fig 47.

Early 18C. Wood. Glazing bar
faces interior.

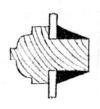

Mid-18C. Laminated wood
contruction.

Mid-18C. Wood. Narrower profile
than early 18C

Last quarter of 18C. Underwood
patent bar. Moulded leaf rib
soldered to metal web.

Post-1780. 'Eldorado' glazing bar.
Cast iron rib crimped to metal
web.

Regency period. 'Lamb's Tongue'
glazing bar. Wood construction.

Lead 'cames' as used in modern
lead-light.

About 1740, the semi-circular fanlight (Fig.48) was predominant. Toplights have occurred c.1720 in a fretted form (Fig.49), but this style lasted little more than ten years, although Lloyd (9) illustrates an example dated c.1750. With insufficient dated examples, stylistic changes in fanlight patterns are difficult to disentangle, with a few exceptions. Fig.31 in the chapter on Doorways illustrates a type popularised by Adam c.1770, and toplights with margins (Fig.50) may coincide with the introduction of margined windows c.1810 (Fig.39).

Fanlights are relatively easy to replace, and so caution must be exercised in dating them. Look for glazing bar thickness, shape, and the direction in which the decorative moulding faces. Try to determine the bar material by feel; wood may feel warmer, and lead or cast iron will be very thin. The sound from a gentle tap with the plastic-covered handle of a Swiss army knife should tell the difference between wood and cast iron.

Bibliography

1. M.S.Briggs, Everyman's Concise Encyclopaedia of Architecture, 1966.
2. R.J.Brown, English Farmhouses, 1985.
3. A.Clifton-Taylor, Six more English Towns, 1986.
4. D. Cruickshank & P. Wyld, Georgian Town Houses and their Details, 1986.
5. P. Cunnington, How Old is Your House? 1982.
6. E. Gray, The British House, 1994.
7. Alexander Stuart Gray, John Sambrook and Charlotte Halliday, Fanlights a visual architectural history. 1990.
8. H.J. Louw, The Origin of the Sash-Window: Architectural History 26, 1983.
9. N. Lloyd, The History of the English House, 1931.
10. S. Muthesius, The English Terraced House, 1990.
11. R.J. Naismith, Buildings of the Scottish Countryside, 1989.
12. L.F. Salzman, Building in England down to 1540, 1967.
13. G. Sheeran, Good Houses Built of Stone, 1986.

14.   J.T. Smith, E.M. Yates, On the Dating of English Houses from External Evidence; Field Studies Vol.2 No.3, 1968.
15.   I. Ware, A Complete Body of Architecture, 1756.
16.   J. Wight, Brick Building in England from the Middle Ages to 1550, 1972.

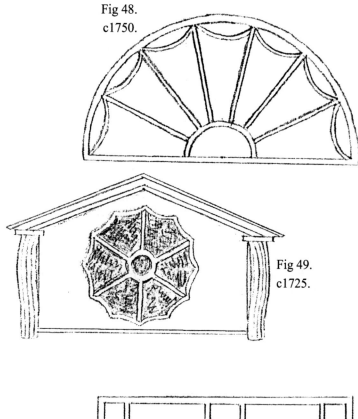

Fig 48.
c1750.

Fig 49.
c1725.

Fig 50.
c1825.

NINETEENTH CENTURY DETAILS

This short chapter is written about the nineteenth century because it was a time of rapidly growing industrialisation, with corresponding increases in population and prosperity, for some, if not all. The universal availability of building materials, made possible by the building of railways, led to the rapid demise of any remaining vernacular traditions of building. In their place came a restless experimentation with different building styles, fuelled by increasing affluence, which led to rapid stylistic changes. For ease of reference, these changes are briefly summarised, at nominal ten-year intervals, through the century. The data has been obtained by personal observation, largely supplemented by information available in Muthesius (2) and Gray (1); both of these references are indispensable.

The scope of this book does not aim to give a guide to the visual dating of houses from the twentieth century, as deeds and other documentary evidence are normally available. However, for the dedicated date- spotter, Gray should be consulted.

1810   Terraces continued to show Georgian style until c.1840.

Verandahs and balconies were popularised in the late eighteenth century and continued to be used to c.1850.

Portland stone was used in much early nineteenth century building.

Margined glazing (see Windows) became common. It continued in use to c.1850, when a change to 'Oxford' glazing took place.

Sixteen-pane sash windows were reintroduced in the late eighteenth century (see Windows) and continued in use to c.1840.

1820 Gothic features were becoming fashionable as a reaction to Georgian plainness. These included much use of gables, pointed arches, squared drip-moulds and decorative bargeboarding on gables. Gothic styles continued to c.1860.

The popularity of brick was at its lowest until c.1840, for external facades. White/grey bricks came into use in East Anglia.

Cast iron decorative details became very popular for the next twenty years. They declined in importance by c.1860.

Flat-topped porches, supported by large columns, were becoming common.

1830 This was the nominal end of the Regency period, and the beginning of Early-Victorian styles. These continued to c.1855.

Horizontal features such as stringcourses began to be favoured in place of vertical details such as pilasters.

Stucco, for external facades, was at its most popular. It gradually became less popular, until c.1870, when it was hardly used at all.

Facades were enriched with many small Italian Renaissance details, to which the term Italian style was loosely applied. Round-arched windows, and asymmetrical facades, little square towers, and elaborate eaves and cornices, were all symptoms of this fashion. However, care is necessary, as some magnificent examples of the Italianate style were built in Knutsford as late as 1900.

Fanlights were going out of use, being replaced by simple rectangular windows above doors.

The introduction of plate glass led to increasing use of 'horns' to reinforce sash windows.

1840 The 'Tudor revival' started c.1845. Elizabethan and Jacobean details were used. Features included prominent gables and large mullioned and transomed windows.

Steep roof pitches became a common fashion. This was probably a revulsion against the very low pitches (30°) which became common c.1820 when Welsh slate became readily available. The low pitches remained in frequent use to c.1850, however.

Bay windows became common in seaside resorts.

Decorative details such as balconies, balustrades, quoins and rusticated stonework were increasingly popular.

1850 Nominal start of High-Victorian styles. c.1855.

Asymmetry.

Texture contrasts - use of rubble walls with ashlar dressings, in place of smooth, uniform ashlar or stucco facades - continued well into 1870's.

Colour contrasts:

- use of strongly coloured stones such as brown York stone or yellow Bath stone.

- use of multi-coloured brickwork. This was popular to c.1890.

Moulded bricks came into use in place of 'rubbed' bricks.

The removal of the duty on plate glass c.1845 probably led to the 'Oxford' style of 'Bordered' glazing (see Windows).

Flemish and Dutch gables came into favour in the north. In the Hexham area there are ten examples concentrated in the period c.1885 to 1899, illustrating the characteristically brief duration and intensity of most fashions.

1860   Decorative features (lintels, quoins etc.) were placed flush with the walls of the building to give an uninterrupted facade - a short-lived fashion.

Multi-coloured surfaces were extremely popular.

Terracotta details such as finials and crestings for the ridges of stone or tiled roofs became affordable for large houses.

Mansard roofs became common - even more so in the 1880's. (French Second Empire style.)

'Snecked' stonework became acceptable in the north east, to enliven facades.

Bay windows came into general use in the suburbs of London.

Mock timber-framing was introduced.

Small, square, stone corbels were used in some areas in the north to support rainwater gutters. A short-lived feature, but of local use in the north.

1870   The 'Queen Anne Revival' started, and continued during the next twenty years. It featured the use of strongly-coloured red brickwork, with white paintwork. Gothic irregularity, and gauged brick arches were also used for this style.

Stucco fell out of use more or less completely.

Pressed white bricks were used from this date in Cambridgeshire.

Bay windows were now common even in very small houses.

Tile hanging on upper floors became common.

Byelaws became effective (1850, 1870) which required floorboards to be raised off the ground to avoid dampness and rot.

1880 Terracotta roof crestings and finials became affordable for medium-sized houses.

Decorative lintels (chamfers etc.) and stone details became s tandard. (See Windows and Masonry.)

Sash windows, with small-pane glazing in the upper sash only, came into use, and remained popular for about thirty years (see Windows).

Mock timber-framing, especially for gables, became common. It was very frequently used by c.1890, and it was used virtually everywhere by 1900, in some part of a building.

The juxtaposition of contrasting materials, for effect, became commonplace. Brick would be contrasted with flint, rubble stonework could be used with ashlar of a different colour, or perhaps with hard-pressed colourful brick.

1890 Roughcast with half-timbering was used on gables.

Pebbledash on walls was becoming increasingly common.

Portland stone was back in favour for large, prestigious buildings.

Stucco had a brief revival of use.

In the Newcastle area, a two-piece window with stone piers between the two parts, and stone lintels, became common (see Windows).

Bibliography

1.   E. Gray, The British House, 1994.
2.   S. Muthesius, The English Terraced House, 1982.

APPENDIX 1

Brick Bond Distribution Over Four Centuries. (After Anthea Brian).

Header Bond

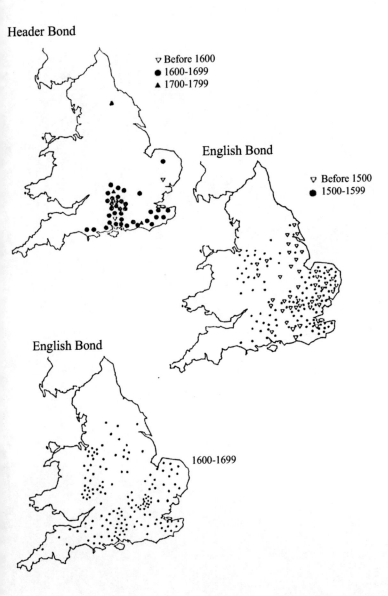

English Bond

English Bond

English Bond

1700-1799

English Garden Bond

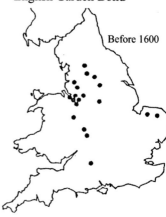

Before 1600

English Garden Bond

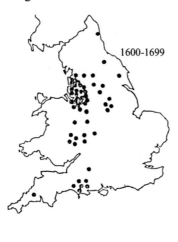

1600-1699

English Garden Bond

1700-1799

Flemish Bond

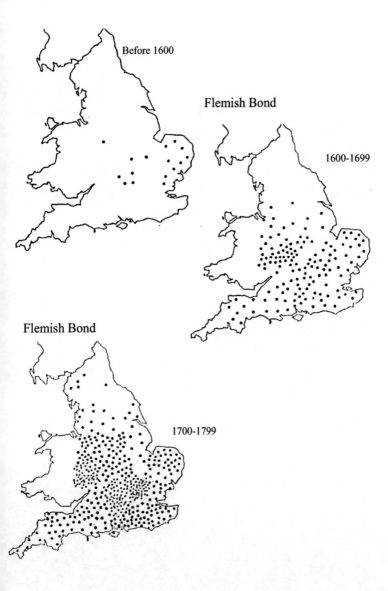

Before 1600

Flemish Bond

1600-1699

Flemish Bond

1700-1799

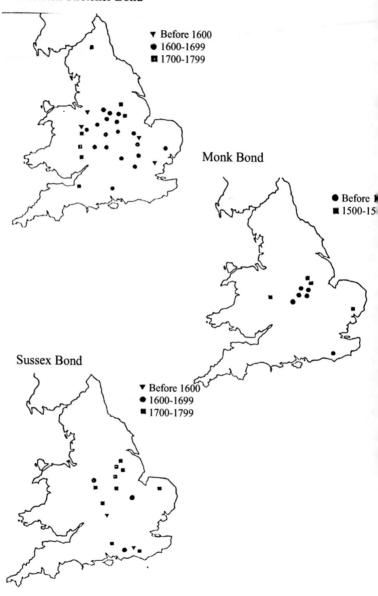

Flemish Stretcher Bond

▼ Before 1600
● 1600-1699
■ 1700-1799

Monk Bond

● Before 1
■ 1500-15

Sussex Bond

▼ Before 1600
● 1600-1699
■ 1700-1799

Index